Garden Way's
Joy of Gardening
HANDBOOK

by Mark Hebert

Garden Way Publishing
Storey Communications, Pownal, Vermont

Cover photo by Didier Delmas
Illustrations by Elayne Sears

Third Printing, June, 1985.

Printed in the United States by Alpine Press.

The name Garden Way Publishing is licensed to Storey Communications, Inc.
by Garden Way, Inc.

Library of Congress Cataloging in Publication Data

Hebert, Mark.
  Garden Way's joy of gardening handbook.

  Includes index.
  1. Vegetable gardening — Handbooks, manuals, etc.
I. Garden Way Publishing. II. Title. III. Title:
Joy of gardening handbook.
SB321.H39 1984   635   83-48974
ISBN 0-88266-357-7

Introduction

A number of years ago I was touring over two acres of the most beautiful vegetable gardens in the world when a strapping young fellow rolled a cart full of freshly harvested vegetables over to us. "Dean, this is Mark Hebert," said Dick Raymond. Mark was about to weigh part of the harvest of a 30 x 40-foot garden that would go on to produce nearly $1,000 worth of vegetables in just one season.

Mark had been working side by side with Dick, and before long he won Dick's confidence and admiration to the point where Dick made him manager of the day-to-day activities of Garden Way's experimental gardens.

Garden Way Gardens is a busy place, and for five years, Mark Hebert has been at the center of that activity. Vegetable gardening is the main focus at the gardens and everywhere, in every shape and size are beautiful, productive examples. Here gardening methods and techniques like wide-row growing and raised beds are tested against other growing methods. New varieties of plants and old favorites are tried in real backyard conditions. Garden tools and equipment are also tested and evaluated to make sure they live up to Garden Way's high standards.

This *Joy of Gardening Handbook,* with its photos, charts and information, brings together in one place the benefits of Mark's years of testing and experiences. It is both a companion to The Joy of Gardening book and a permanent log for the home gardener.

Mark views it all with a critical eye, recording successes and failures and analyzing the "why" of it. And sharing what he has learned with gardeners everywhere.

His gardening experience began as a youngster, when he was growing up in a market growing area near Burlington, Vermont. He earned pocket money by picking beans for a quarter a bushel, then went home and worked in his own plot in the family garden. "Kids today might laugh at a quarter for that much work," says Mark, "but it taught me some important lessons about gardening and working for a living."

Today, Mark's interests are focused in the garden but range into related areas. He is an accomplished writer and photographer, and his words and photos have appeared in several national magazines that go into millions of homes of America's gardeners and homemakers. Working with radar during a tour of duty in Viet Nam, he developed an interest in meteorology and he now enjoys keeping a detailed weather log. Gardening also led to an interest in beekeeping, and he keeps several hives "just for fun" near the garden at his home in rural Vermont. A home he built himself. A constant tinkerer, Mark has a knack for putting things together. Need a greenhouse? Cold frame? Trellis? Garden shed? No problem. In fact, the barn-roofed garden shed on the cover of this book—it is also the basic set for the Joy of Gardening television series—began its life as a rough sketch and a pile of material in the driveway. When Popular Mechanics magazine saw a photo of the shed they featured it as a do-it-yourself project, and followed it up with plans for the greenhouse and root cellar at the gardens. And later an article on simple garden structures.

Now, with the production of the Joy of Gardening television series, life at Garden Way Gardens has taken a new turn. Through the series, which now

Raising fruit trees is also important to Mark Hebert.

Photo by Paul Boisvert

is available to about half the homes in the country, Mark is able to share his gardening know-how with a huge audience.

Behind the scenes, Mark is responsible for the massive planning effort that goes into making sure the Gardens and the cameras are ready at the same time—a shooting schedule that begins in April and ends in October. The planning begins in December when the topics of the thirteen half-hour programs are firmed up and gardens are designed to match the topics and the shooting schedule. Meanwhile, the testing of everything involved in backyard gardening continues. There's even a test garden in Florida, so the outdoor season never ends.

Keeping track of everything is a big job. That's why nobody is better qualified to pull together a book like this than Mark Hebert.

"It's amazing how keeping good garden notes can make you a better gardener," says Mark. "It's all right there in front of you, there's no need to rely on your memory. You can eliminate those things that just don't work for you and improve those that do."

With this book, Mark shares his secrets for creating successful gardens every year, and I know you'll enjoy both the book and the results that follow.

Dean Leith, Jr.

Dean Leith, Jr.

4

This Is Your Book

By working together in the following pages, you and I can create a gardening book that is uniquely yours.

It will be a record of your successes, which varieties were tastiest, what methods worked best for you, that will help you in future gardens.

It's your personal guide and a three-year record, so that you can use it for years to come. Which of those tomato varieties did you like best? You started those melons inside a bit too early—but on what date? You planted three long rows of strawberries, each a different variety. Which variety did you put where?

You'll have the answers to these and hundreds of other questions right at your fingertips in this book.

Jot Everything Down

And it won't be much trouble, either. Just mark things down as you do them, from buying seeds to harvest time. A friend of mine keeps one of these record books right in his garden. He put a mailbox on a pole. Inside are the book and a pen. The pages sometimes get a bit dirty, but the record is there, ready to help him.

The first step to take is to write down, on the line below, the dates for the average last spring frost and the first fall frost in your area. If you don't know them, estimate from the maps on pages 28 and 29, or get advice from a fellow gardener, the Extension Service, or the Weather Service.

_____

Last Spring Frost Date   First Fall Frost Date

Now turn to page 6, and list the crops you plan to grow, and when you plan to start them, under *Scheduled Planting.*

On the next page, note the actual frost dates and any other weather conditions, such as dry spells, as they occur. Also list your gardening expenses. Then draw your garden plan as you set out transplants or sow seeds, and write down, under the separate vegetable listings, what varieties you planted, when, and how. Use the "days to maturity" information and plan when you expect the harvest to begin. This is handy. By figuring ahead, you can keep from having a heavy crop of beans ready just as you take off for two weeks of vacation. Or you can figure when you want to do your canning and freezing, and plant accordingly.

Remember your preference, and that's about it, until harvesting time. You'll want to write down then when you started picking. Most important, while it's fresh in your mind, you'll want to make a note of each crop and how you liked it. Too much Swiss chard? Not enough onions? Didn't like that early corn? You loved those early Pixie tomatoes? Write them all down, and you won't forget, next January, when you're making out your list of seeds to buy.

PLANTING SCHEDULE SUMMARY
FIRST YEAR, 19 _94_

Crop	Scheduled Planting		Actual Planting	
	Date Started Indoors	Date Transplanted Or Seeds Outdoors	Date Started Indoors	Date Transplanted Or Seeds Outdoors
3 - tomato				
13 tomatoes				5/20/94
12 cukes				✓
10 peppers				✓

FIRST YEAR'S GARDENING, 19 ____

Last spring frost _____   *First fall frost* _____

Notes on season's weather _____

_____

_____

Problems, achievements _____

_____

_____

YEAR'S EXPENSES

Items	Cost	Items	Cost
Seeds _____	_____	*Tools, Supplies* _____	_____
_____	_____	_____	_____
_____	_____	_____	_____
_____	_____	_____	_____
_____	_____	_____	_____
_____	_____	_____	_____
_____	_____	_____	_____
Plants _____	_____	_____	_____
_____	_____	_____	_____
_____	_____	_____	_____
_____	_____	_____	_____
_____	_____	_____	_____
_____	_____	_____	_____
_____	_____	_____	_____
Fertilizer, Mulch _____	_____	_____	_____
_____	_____	*Other expenses* _____	_____
_____	_____	_____	_____
_____	_____	_____	_____
_____	_____	_____	_____
_____	_____	_____	_____
Total _____		*Total* _____	

Total for Year _____

7

FIRST YEAR 19 _____
INITIAL PLANTING

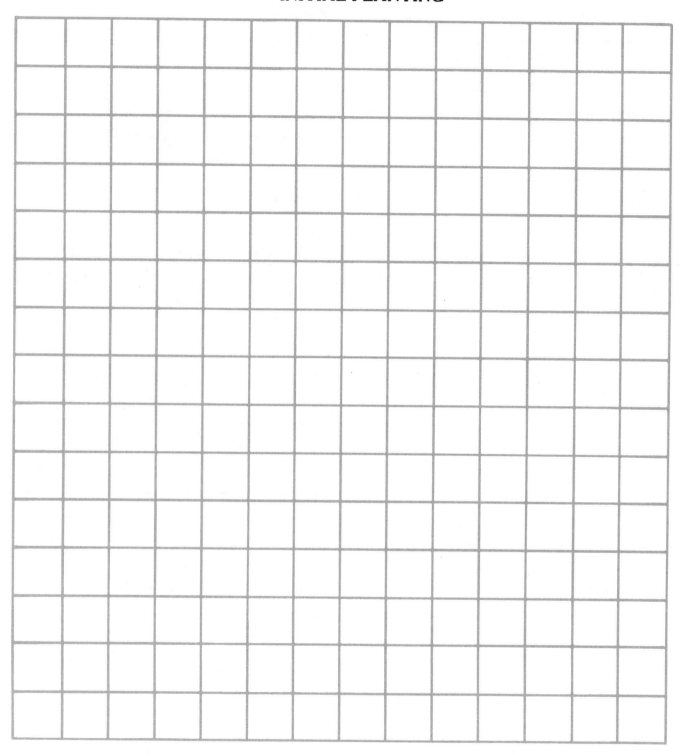

Select a scale that fits your garden plan. Each square here measures a half-inch.

FIRST YEAR 19 _____
LATER PLANTING

Select a scale that fits your garden plan. Each square here measures a half-inch.

PLANTING SCHEDULE SUMMARY
SECOND YEAR, 19 _____

Crop	Scheduled Planting		Actual Planting	
	Date Started Indoors	Date Transplanted Or Seeds Outdoors	Date Started Indoors	Date Transplanted Or Seeds Outdoors
_____	_____	_____	_____	_____
_____	_____	_____	_____	_____
_____	_____	_____	_____	_____
_____	_____	_____	_____	_____
_____	_____	_____	_____	_____
_____	_____	_____	_____	_____
_____	_____	_____	_____	_____
_____	_____	_____	_____	_____
_____	_____	_____	_____	_____
_____	_____	_____	_____	_____
_____	_____	_____	_____	_____
_____	_____	_____	_____	_____
_____	_____	_____	_____	_____
_____	_____	_____	_____	_____
_____	_____	_____	_____	_____
_____	_____	_____	_____	_____
_____	_____	_____	_____	_____
_____	_____	_____	_____	_____
_____	_____	_____	_____	_____
_____	_____	_____	_____	_____
_____	_____	_____	_____	_____
_____	_____	_____	_____	_____
_____	_____	_____	_____	_____
_____	_____	_____	_____	_____
_____	_____	_____	_____	_____
_____	_____	_____	_____	_____
_____	_____	_____	_____	_____

SECOND YEAR'S GARDENING, 19 ____

Last spring frost _____ *First fall frost* _____

Notes on season's weather _____

_____

_____

Problems, achievements _____

_____

_____

YEAR'S EXPENSES

Items	Cost	Items	Cost
Seeds _____	_____	*Tools, Supplies* _____	_____
_____	_____	_____	_____
_____	_____	_____	_____
_____	_____	_____	_____
_____	_____	_____	_____
_____	_____	_____	_____
Plants _____	_____	_____	_____
_____	_____	_____	_____
_____	_____	_____	_____
_____	_____	_____	_____
_____	_____	_____	_____
Fertilizer, Mulch _____	_____	_____	_____
_____	_____	*Other expenses* _____	_____
_____	_____	_____	_____
_____	_____	_____	_____
_____	_____	_____	_____
	Total _____		*Total* _____

Total for Year _____

11

SECOND YEAR 19 _____
INITIAL PLANTING

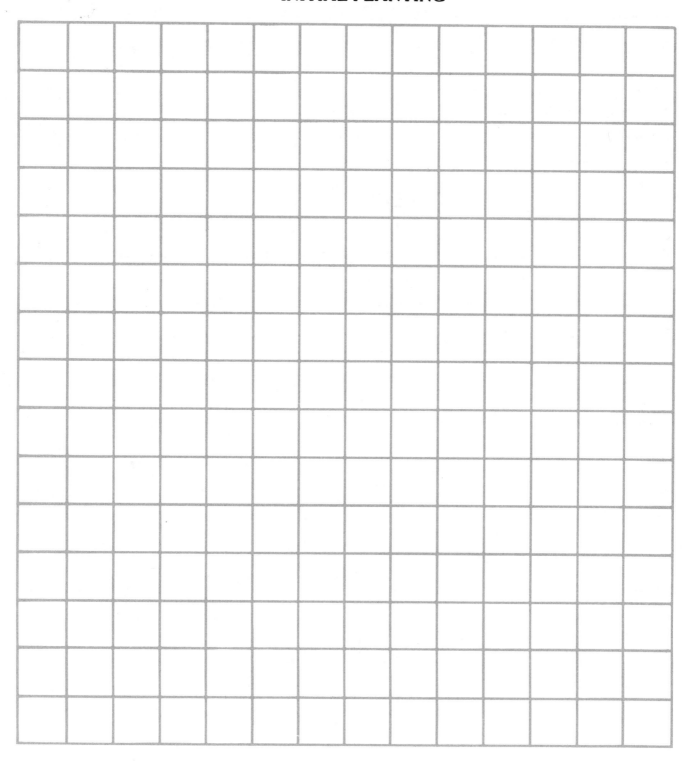

Select a scale that fits your garden plan. Each square here measures a half-inch.

SECOND YEAR 19 _____
LATER PLANTING

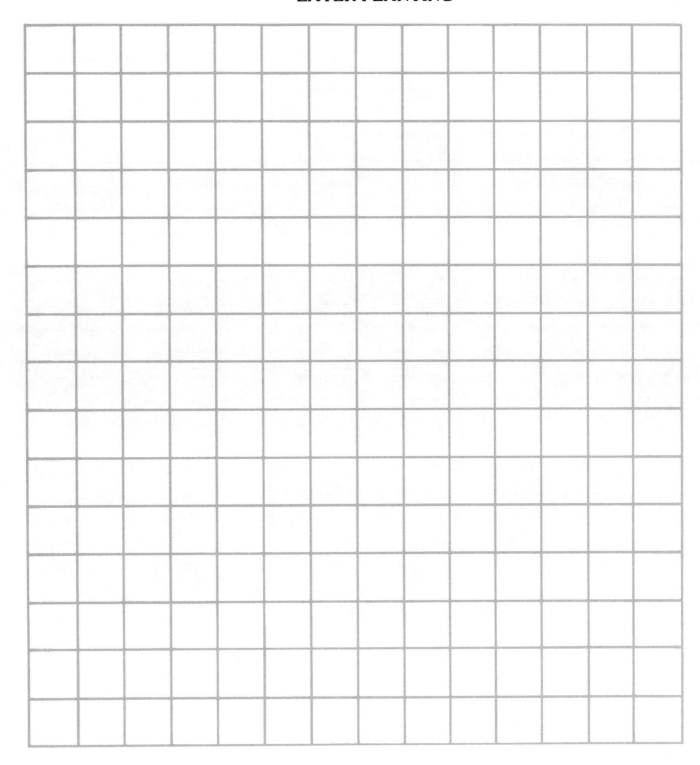

Select a scale that fits your garden plan. Each square here measures a half-inch.

PLANTING SCHEDULE SUMMARY
THIRD YEAR, 19 _____

Crop	Scheduled Planting		Actual Planting	
	Date Started Indoors	Date Transplanted Or Seeds Outdoors	Date Started Indoors	Date Transplanted Or Seeds Outdoors

14

THIRD YEAR'S GARDENING, 19 ____

Last spring frost _____ *First fall frost* _____

Notes on season's weather _____
_____
_____

Problems, achievements _____
_____
_____

YEAR'S EXPENSES

Items	Cost	Items	Cost
Seeds _____	_____	*Tools, Supplies* _____	_____
_____	_____	_____	_____
_____	_____	_____	_____
_____	_____	_____	_____
_____	_____	_____	_____
_____	_____	_____	_____
Plants _____	_____	_____	_____
_____	_____	_____	_____
_____	_____	_____	_____
_____	_____	_____	_____
_____	_____	_____	_____
_____	_____	_____	_____
Fertilizer, Mulch _____	_____	_____	_____
_____	_____	*Other expenses* _____	_____
_____	_____	_____	_____
_____	_____	_____	_____
_____	_____	_____	_____
Total _____		*Total* _____	

Total for Year _____

15

THIRD YEAR 19 _____
INITIAL PLANTING

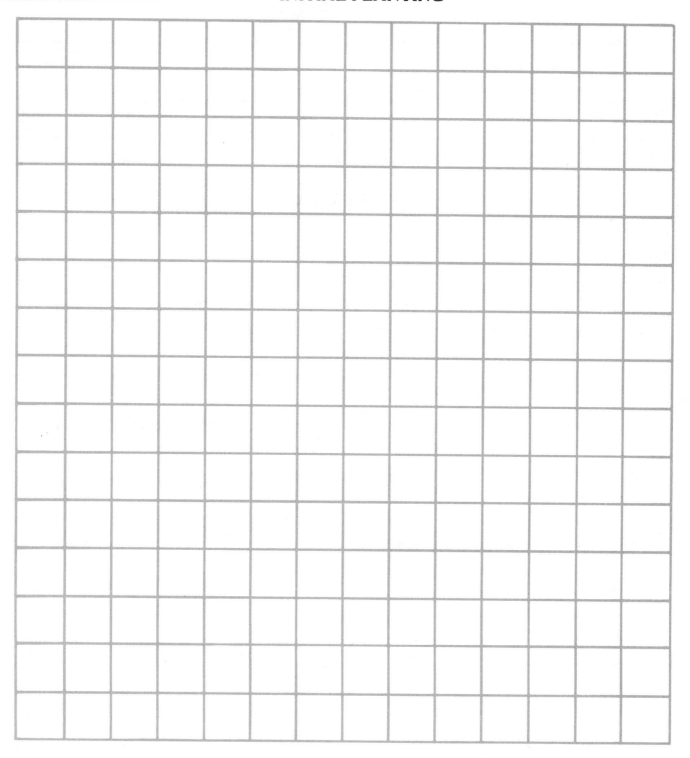

Select a scale that fits your garden plan. Each square here measures a half-inch.

THIRD YEAR 19 _____
LATER PLANTING

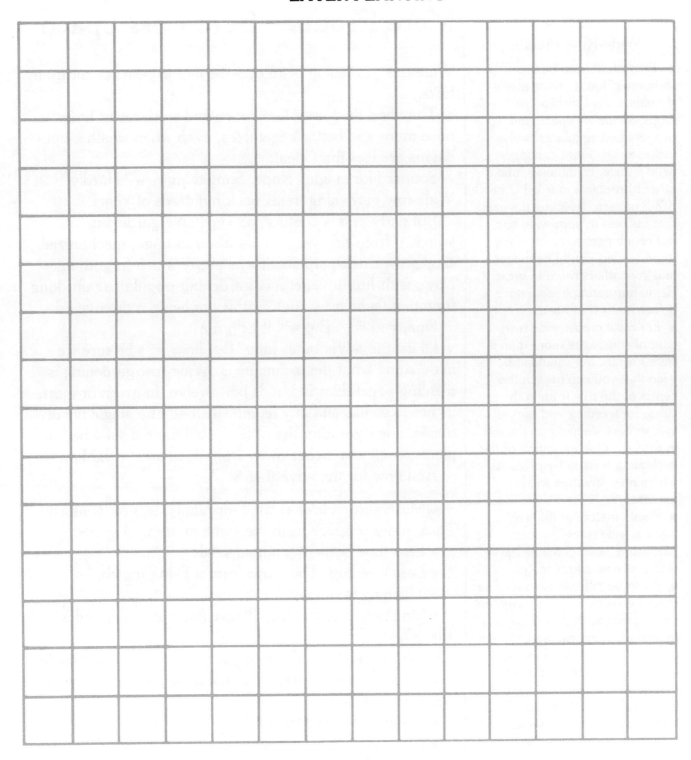

Select a scale that fits your garden plan. Each square here measures a half-inch.

- Transplants can be grown in wide rows, too. Lettuce plants should be eight inches apart, cole crops ten inches apart, and peppers and eggplants twelve inches apart. Plant cabbages, head lettuce, cauliflower, and other transplants in a 2-1-2 or a 3-2-3 pattern, selecting the one that fits best in your wide row.
- For a bigger harvest, enjoy those tender, young cabbages and give others room to grow. Begin harvesting head lettuce before it has firm heads.
- For most crops, wide rows can, of course, be more than a rake's width, but shouldn't be so wide that you can't reach the center of the row from both sides, for weeding and harvesting, without stepping on the soil in the bed. One exception of this is planting peas in large blocks, where no cultivation will be necessary.
- Plants mature at different rates in wide rows. So start harvesting and continue harvesting as new plants mature.
- It can be difficult to space fine seeds correctly, so often they end up planted too thickly. However, thinning is easy with an ordinary garden rake. When plants are just an inch tall, drag the rake across the row with the teeth in the soil about half an inch. This removes some of the plants, leaving room for the others to grow. This also loosens the soil within the row and destroys many newly sprouted weeds.

Wide-Row Gardening:
More Produce from Less Space

Wide-row gardening is an eye-opening experience for many folks.

They find they need less space and work fewer hours to raise more and better vegetables, even when weather conditions are less than ideal.

Sounds like magic? Nope. Something new? Hardly. Wide-row gardening dates back hundreds of years.

But early in this century, as vegetable gardening switched from an every-family affair to huge, mechanized, single-row truck gardens, it was pretty much forgotten. Now, with home vegetable gardening popular again, long-forgotten techniques such as this are being rediscovered.

Fine, you say. But will it help me?

I'll list the advantages later. But first, let's be sure we understand what the technique is. Wide-row gardening is planting vegetables in bands ten, twelve, fourteen or more inches in width, and any length. Instead of a single file of plants, one right after the other, you'll have a solid bed of plants, each just inches away from its nearest neighbor.

And now for the advantages:

- More garden area is used for plants, less for walkways. Thus, more produce from the same amount of space.
- Less time is spent planting seeds.
- Less weeding. The crops form a living mulch.
- Thinning is simple.
- Moisture is conserved. Plants shade the soil, and it dries slowly.
- In mid-summer, with crops shading the soil, it is cooler.
- Harvesting is easier. You pick a lot without moving up and down a row.
- Longer harvest period.
- Avoids problem of soil compaction close to plants, so plants grow better.

How to Plant a Wide Row

Start with a loose, fertile seedbed.

Garden soil is loaded with weed seeds. Those near the surface will germinate.

Working the soil moves seeds to the germination zone where they sprout.

Work the soil several times. Many seeds will germinate, leaving fewer to trouble you later.

1. *Mark edge of row with string.* Don't walk in row. Work from one side of it.

2. *Mark width of row* by drawing a garden rake alongside the string. The width of the rake—about sixteen inches—is ideal. Dragging the rake down the wide row also removes debris and smoothes and levels the seedbed.

3. *Fertilize* the row area, if it's necessary. Use two cups of commercial fertilizer such as 5-10-10 for every ten feet of row, or four cups of dehydrated manure. Add high-phosphorus fertilizer, such as bone meal, for root crops and onions. Rake in fertilizer, then smooth soil with back of rake.

4. *Broadcast seeds.* Sprinkle them evenly over the length and width of the row, like grass seed. Don't worry too much about spacing, but better to sow too thickly. Plants can be thinned easily later on. Here are two planting tips: Sprinkle in a few radish seeds. They're good companion plants. First, they'll germinate and mark the wide row.

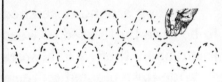

Pattern for broadcasting seeds.

Then, as you harvest them, they will loosen the soil. Large seeds are easy to space correctly, but small seeds can be tricky. I use a discarded spice shaker bottle, such as the one used for garlic powder. It makes a great wide-row seeder.

5. *Firm seeds* down with the back of a hoe or rake.

6. *Cover seeds* with soil to four times their diameter. That's about one inch for large seeds such as peas and beans, a quarter-inch to a half-inch for small ones such as lettuce and carrots. Pull soil from beyond the row, lift it into the center of the seedbed, then, using the back of a rake, level it over the seeds.

7. *Tamp down seedbed* with hoe or rake so seeds make good contact with the soil.

Until the seedings come up, keep the seedbed moist. If a crust forms on clay, drag a rake gently over it to break up the crust.

Wide-Row Gardening

Here are just some of the crops that grow well in wide rows. You may want to try others.

Beans	Chard	Lettuce	Peppers
Beets	Collards	Mustard	Radishes
Cabbage	Endive	Onions	Rutabagas
Carrots	Kale	Parsnips	Spinach
Cauliflower	Kohlrabi	Peas	Turnips

And here are the vegetables that don't grow as well, so we recommend that you don't try the wide-row method with them.

Corn	Melons	Pumpkins	Tomatoes
Cucumber	Potatoes	Squash	

Raised Beds Are Problem-Solvers

Planting Hints

• If the weather is dry when planting, keep seedbed moist until seeds germinate.

• In South, particularly, mulch sides of beds heavily to hold in moisture during hot, dry summers.

• To weed walkway and sides of bed, use tiller with hilling attachment, or work with a hoe.

• If you have soil that is too damp, but you want to raise corn, form raised beds and plant double rows of corn. Later, hill corn as usual to support stalks as they grow.

• Raised beds warm up faster in spring, stay warmer. Great for heat-loving plants like peppers, tomatoes, eggplant, and okra.

Raised beds are the gardener's problem-solvers.

Do you have heavy clay soil that takes weeks to dry out in the spring? Form raised beds in the fall and you won't waste all that warm weather that's so good for just-planted gardens.

Low-lying areas? Their extra moisture can be a plus if it surrounds raised beds. Eager for warm soil in the spring, to plant melons, lima beans, and other heat-loving plants? Raised beds heat up more quickly than flat areas of soil. And dry out much more quickly after flash rains that might wash the seeds from conventional plantings. Rain water doesn't puddle on top of raised beds.

These beds are also good in the garden with a very thin layer of topsoil, doubling the amount available to the plants, and making it possible to raise fine root crops.

Working around raised beds is a delight. You don't have to bend so far to seed or weed or harvest from them, and maintaining them is light work with a hoe.

Wide rows planted on raised beds have all the advantages I listed on page 18. I'm sure you will discover more advantages yourself.

Next season, try at least one raised bed. Carrots, maybe, or beets, or onions. You'll find that raised beds are the jewels of your vegetable garden, and you'll want to try more the next year.

Making Raised Beds

Once you have the knack of it, making raised beds is a snap. Here are two methods, one using hand tools, the other using a rear-end tiller.

Using Hand Tools

1. Prepare a deep, loose seedbed. If it's needed, add compost or fertilizer, or both, to the bed, and mix into the top few inches of soil.

2. Mark the bed with stakes and strings. The size is up to you, but for the first trial, you might mark out a bed that would be about sixteen inches wide, so space strings about thirty-six inches apart. The top of the bed can be elevated six to ten inches above the walkway, and the bed walls will slope toward the walkway. Experiment to get dimensions with which you can be comfortable.

3. Pull soil from walkway to the top of the bed. Using a rake, move along one walkway, pulling four to six inches of soil from the opposite walkway. Repeat the process from the other side. Make a pile of the soil. Pile it high. The deeper, the better.

4. Level top of the bed, using the back of the rake.

5. Plant, using the method described under How to Plant a Wide Row.

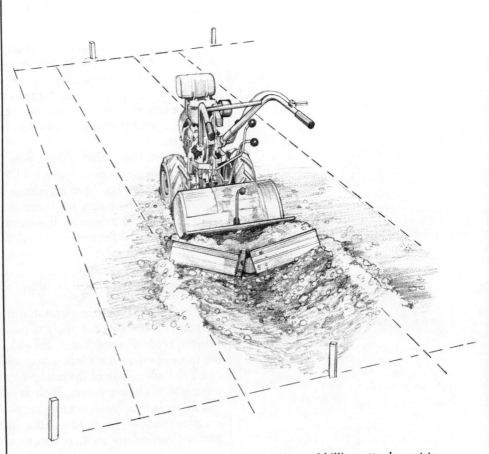

Set stakes two tiller widths apart. Attach furrowing and hilling attachment to tiller. Line up center of the tiller in front of one stake, then till to other stake. Continue this to form beds and walkways.

Using a Tiller

1. Prepare a deep, loose seedbed. Add fertilizer or compost if needed.

2. Stake out tiller route, to form walkways. Set stakes at each end of the row two tiller widths apart.

3. Attach furrowing and hilling attachment to tiller. Set hilling wings to the highest position so they'll push a lot of soil upward onto the bed.

4. Hill up beds. Line up center of tiller in front of the first stake, point it at stake at other end of bed, and guide tiller directly toward it. At other end, repeat with next two stakes.

5. Smooth the bed top with a rake.

6. Plant, using steps four through seven under How to Plant a Wide Row.

Rotating in the Garden

You can improve your garden soil and lessen your problems with disease and insects by rotating your garden crops each year.

Think of this when you lay out this year's garden in the pages provided for it. And refer to your plan for rotating in the following years. That's what makes a record of your garden layout so valuable; you don't have to depend on your memory as you decide where to put those tomato plants next year.

Gardeners often select a three-year cycle for their gardens, which fits well with the three years of use planned for this book.

Rotating crops has been a practice on farmland for centuries. It's impossible, however, to design a rotation plan for a vegetable garden that will work as smoothly as one for the many acres of a farm. The difference is the number of vegetables grown in a relatively small area.

However, it is possible to gain some of the advantages of rotating, even in the smallest of gardens.

Here are some things to consider.

• Don't plant the same vegetable in the same location, year after year. And don't follow any members of the cabbage family—cabbage, Brussels sprouts, broccoli, cauliflower, collards, kohlrabi, and others—with others of the same family. That's how insect and soil problems get started.

• Take advantage of the nitrogen-collectors, peas and beans, and follow them with the heavy eaters, such as corn.

• Squeeze in a green manure crop—beans, peas, soybeans, buckwheat, ryegrass, annual rye, or any of the others—when you have space in the garden. Particularly try to plant one at the end of the gardening season.

Inoculating Seeds

Legumes, which include peas and beans, have the ability to attract certain soil bacteria to their roots. These bacteria can extract nitrogen from the air and convert it to a form usable by plants. The peas and beans benefit from the extra nitrogen now, and future crops get a boost after the legumes are turned under.

To make certain these bacteria are present, you can inoculate legume seeds with these tiny creatures before planting. The inoculant, which looks like a dark powder, can be purchased at garden stores. Make certain you buy the special strain for beans and peas, if that is what you are inoculating. There are others, for various clovers and for soybeans, for example.

Follow directions for inoculating the seeds. They're printed on the container. It's simple, usually adding water to the inoculant, then mixing the seeds into it. Do it just before planting the seeds.

Taking the Mystery Out of pH

You can make pH as complicated or as simple as you want to.

Let's make it simple. pH is a measure of the acidity or alkalinity of the soil.

Ideally the pH reading in a garden is 6.5-6.8, which is slightly on the low (or acid) side of a neutral reading of 7. Some crops such as watermelons and potatoes prefer a reading around 6. Blueberries, too, like an acid soil.

You find the pH yourself by making a test with a simple kit you can buy, or learn it as part of a complete soil test by an independent laboratory or the Cooperative Extension Service.

If the pH reading is too low, you can add lime. If high, or too sweet, you add suplhur, aluminum sulphate, or iron sulphate. The boxes on this page tell how much.

You'll see some gardening books that get very specific about pH. They will advise 7 for asparagus, 6.5 for peas, and 6 for carrots, for example. And the poor gardener has nightmares of testing and testing until each row is exactly right.

That's making it complicated. Aim for a range of about 6.5-6.8, slightly less if you're raising potatoes. The reason for a lower reading for the potato land is that this discourages the scab that can make potatoes look so unsightly.

You have questions, and they're good ones. Why all this fuss about pH? If it takes a chemistry set to figure it out, how will the plants know? Why not make sure the soil is rich with organic materials and is well tilled, and let it go at that?

The answer is that a soil that's too sweet or sour, that has a reading far from 6.5, "locks up" some of the nutrients, such as phosphorus.

The plants need the nutrients, they're there in the soil, but the plants can't absorb them. This is the reason why adding lime to an acid soil often can produce as dramatic changes in the plants as adding nutrients. Those nutrients are "unlocked," made available to the plants, and suddenly there's a spurt in growth.

Lime or sulfur can be added to the soil at any time. Many add these when clearing the garden and planting a cover crop in the fall; others do this before tilling the soil in the spring. Either is fine.

We're seeing one problem in our area. Many more families are burning wood to heat their homes. They have lots of wood ashes, and know these ashes are a good source of potassium as well as a substitute for lime. So they dump on the ashes, lots of them. Result: in an area where soils are usually too acid, these soils swing the other way.

My recommendation: don't spread more than one or two ten-quart pails of ashes each year on each 1,000 square feet of garden space. Pound for pound, hardwood ashes are more alkaline than ground limestone.

TO RAISE SOIL ONE UNIT OF pH

	Hydrated Lime	Dolomite	Ground Limestone
Light Soil 100 sq. ft.	1½ lbs.	2 lbs.	2½ lbs.
Heavy Soil 100 sq. ft.	3½ lbs.	5½ lbs.	6 lbs.

TO LOWER SOIL ONE UNIT OF pH

	Sulfur	Aluminum Sulphate	Iron Sulphate
Light Soil 100 sq. ft.	½ lb.	2½ lbs.	3 lbs.
Heavy Soil 100 sq. ft.	2 lbs.	6½ lbs.	7½ lbs.

Note: The amount of lime you use doesn't have to be as precisely measured as this chart suggests.

Special Gardens For Special Purposes

If your vegetable garden has a bit of space left over, and you want to try something different, how about one of these gardens?

Spaghetti Sauce Garden

This is my favorite, because everyone in our family loves spaghetti.

I raise everything for the sauce in one garden—tomatoes, onions, garlic, peppers, oregano, basil, and thyme. Before you select crops for your spaghetti sauce garden, check your favorite recipe. I time my planting so everything matures at the same time, and we put up a big batch every fall.

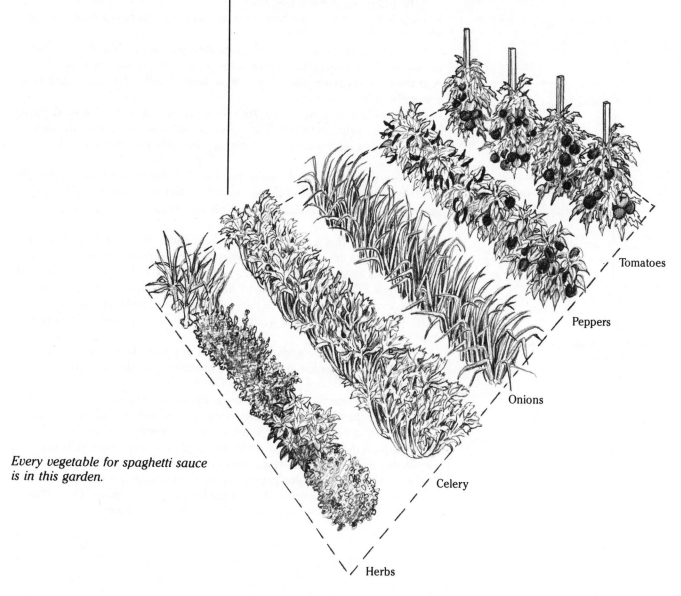

Every vegetable for spaghetti sauce is in this garden.

Tomatoes

Peppers

Onions

Celery

Herbs

The Just-Peas Garden

This for the gardening family that moans, "We never have enough peas." As early in the season as you can work the soil, measure an area ten by ten feet or any convenient size. Prepare it well, tilling and fertilizing it. Then scatter the peas on it, one pound per 100 square feet. Little Marvels and Progress 9 both have short vines, and so are good choices. Rake or till them under. And that's it. The peas will pop up and shade out most of the weeds. The vines will support each other. And when the peas are ready, move in with pails for the picking. You'll trample a few vines, but no matter. You'll harvest fifty pounds or more. And when they're all picked, till in the vines. They're great for enriching the soil. Wait a few days, then plant some other crop.

The Child's Garden

Make it small the first year, so the fledgling gardener doesn't get discouraged. Plant what *the child*, not you, wants to grow. If the child wants some suggestions, here they are:

Pumpkins, for Halloween (but they do take up space), radishes (a quick crop the family can praise the gardener for), carrots (most kids love them raw), peanuts (they grow most peculiarly, and they're easy to grow, and fun to dig up at harvest time).

The Herb Garden

Use your imagination. A border garden. A circle with the herbs in piece-of-pie sections. A tiny garden, near the kitchen door. A raised bed, framed in weathered timbers. A five-by-five-foot space will provide herbs enough for a family. Herbs complement the flavor of food. If you use them, why not grow your own? They're easy.

Stretching the Seasons Means More Produce

There's a tradition among many gardeners in our area—plant your garden on Memorial Day. Everything goes in that day—onion sets, carrot seeds, tomato and pepper plants, everything.

Result is the feast-and-famine harvest. All of a sudden, lots of lettuce, then none. The beans all ripen at once.

If you're one of these gardeners, you're missing opportunities to enjoy tender, early lettuce, to give those onions a good start before the last frost, and to raise the sweetest peas.

There are many opportunities, too, for fall gardening. Late-planted lettuce, kale, cabbage, Brussels sprouts, beets, turnips, broccoli, cauliflower, carrots, Swiss chard, peas, spinach, and rutabagas will all grow after the first frost, providing delicious garden-to-table meals well into the fall.

Even frost-tender vegetables can be started late, giving you last-of-the-season crops of beans, tomatoes, and others. The accompanying table will give you an idea of when to start all of these.

If you want to be more specific, there's a way to figure on how to get a crop of a certain vegetable before the first frost. It's simple arithmetic, starting with the first frost date, and working backward. Here's an example, using beans.

First frost date	October 15
MINUS crops may take longer to mature in fall, 14 days	
MINUS days to maturity (on seed packet), 55 days	
TOTAL days to substract, 69	
Last days to plant beans	August 9

All of this figuring means that if you plant beans on or before August 9, you should have a harvest of fresh beans before the frost lays them low.

Hardy plants survive that first frost, so just count back from first frost date for them.

FALL PLANTING DATES

Fall Harvest	Weeks to plant before first frost	Fall Harvest	Weeks to plant before first frost
Beans	7-10	Head lettuce *	8-10
Beets	8-12	Kale	4-10
Broccoli *	6-8	Lettuce	6-10
Brussels sprouts *	10-12	Mustard	6-10
Cabbage *	6-8	Peas	6-10
Carrots	8-12	Radishes	2-8
Cauliflower *	6-8	Spinach	4-6
Chinese cabbage	6-8	Tomatoes *	8-12
Collards *	6-10		

* Dates given indicate time to transplant seedlings. (These can be started earlier directly in the garden, or in flats or planters outside the garden.)

It's Easy to Start Your Own Seedlings

WHEN TO SOW VEGETABLE SEEDS INDOORS

Crop	Weeks before setting out
Onions, leeks	10-12
Celery	8-10
Tomatoes	6-8
Eggplant	6-8
Peppers	4-6
Cabbage	4-6
Cauliflower	4-6
Broccoli	4-6
Head lettuce	3-4
Melons & cucumbers (separate pots)	3-4

Start your gardening season by starting your own transplants—flowers and vegetables—indoors.

You can time your planting so they're just the right size the day you want to set them out. By starting your own plants, you have a far greater choice of varieties. And, if you follow a few suggestions, you'll have strong, stocky, healthy plants that haven't been under stress, and so will continue to grow fast and strong when you set them out.

If you need another reason for starting transplants, it's a good feeling to work with soil (even if it's not soil but a potting mix) when winter winds still howl, to see the first, fragile leaves unfold, and to smell the living plants.

You can start plants in a sunny window, but you'll have better results because of higher light levels if you rig up something like the one shown, using a half-sheet of plywood, a couple of sawhorses, and three ordinary four-foot fluorescent units, hung so you can raise them. You'll want to keep them just one to two inches above the plants as they grow.

Use flats, peat pots, pyramid planters, or milk cartons as containers. Fill them nearly full with the moist starting mix, sow the seeds (one inch apart for most), firm them into place, cover with soil (¼ inch is plenty for fine seeds), and cover the container in plastic wrap to hold in the moisture, or put the whole flat inside a plastic bag. Place under the lights. Unwrap only when the first seedlings pop into sight.

Water them gently at first, and give them a weekly feeding of liquid houseplant food.

Be sure to harden off plants before placing them in the garden. It takes about a week. Cut back on watering. Put them outdoors in the shade for a few hours on a mild day, and leave them longer the next. Then move them into sunlight. After a few days they can stay out overnight, if there's no threat of frost. Then they're ready for the garden.

Hundreds of seedlings can be started using this arrangement and four-foot fluorescent units.

WIDE ROW PLANTING GUIDE

W/R Crop	Hardiness	Seeds/Plants Amt Per Person	Length Of W/R Per Person	Distance Between Seeds/Plants T = Transplants	Depth To Plant Seeds	Days To Harvest	Tips & Suggestions
Bean	C	¼#	10'-15'	3"-6"	1"	50-60	All but pole varieties do great in wide rows
Beet	B	Pkt	2'-3'	2"-4"	½"	40-80	Eat thinnings-greens and tender young roots are delicious.
Broccoli	A	4-6 plants	4'-6'	16'-18'T	¼"	50-80	Stagger plants in wide row or use 2-1-2 pattern.
Brussels Sprouts	A	3-4 plants	4'-6'	18'-24'T	¼"	90-100	Plant same as above. Best grown as a fall crop.
Cabbage	A	4-5 plants	2'3'	10"-12"T	¼"	60-100	3-2-3 Pattern in 20" wide row provides big harvest
Carrot	B	Pkt	2'-3'	2"-3"	¼"	55-80	Plant in wide rows on raised bed for best carrots ever.
Cauliflower	B	4-6 plants	2'-3'	10"-12"T	¼"	50-80	Plant in 3-2-3 pattern like cabbage.
Collards	A	3-5 plants	2'-5'	16"-18"T	¼"	60-70	Good fall crop but does well in warm or cool weather.
Eggplant	C	2-3 plants	1"	12"-14"T	½"	60-80	Plant in 2-1-2 pattern. Likes warm weather.
Kale	A	½ Pkt	2'-3"	6"-8"	¼"	50-65	Frost improves flavor. Stays green and tasty all winter long.
Kohlrabi	A	½ Pkt	2'-3'	3"-5"	¼"	45-60	Harvest when small, 2"-3" diameter. Big ones are tough, woody.
Lettuce, head	B	8-10 plants	2'-3'	8"-10"T	¼"	60-75	Plant in 3-2-3 pattern for big yields in small spaces.
Lettuce, leaf	B	Pkt	2'-3'	2"-3"	¼"	40-50	Plant short sections often for continuous harvest of sweet lettuce.
Mustard	A	Pkt	3'-5'	2"-3"	¼"	35-45	Fast growing, tasty green, is a great crop North or South.
Onion	A	1# sets / ½ Pkt seed	3'-6' / 2'-3'	2"-4" / 2"-3"	Depth of set / ¼"	30-100 / 60-120	Plant seed and sets close together. Use thinnings for scallions.
Parsley	B	½ Pkt	2'-3'	3"-5"	¼"	70-90	Slow to germinate. A few plants is plenty for most families.
Parsnip	B	Pkt	3'-5'	3"-4"	¼"	100-120	Frost improves flavor. Stores in ground over winter. Harvest in spring.
Peas	A	½#	10'-15'	2"-3"	1"	60-80	In wide rows bush varieties need no support
Pepper	C	6-8 plants	3'-4'	10"-12"T	¼"	60-100	Plant in 2-1-2 pattern for beautiful, productive row.
Radish	A	Pkt	3'-5'	1"-2"	¼"	25-35	Can be sown among other crops to save space.
Rutabaga	A	Pkt	3'-5'	4"-6"	½"	80-90	Best grown as fall crop.
Spinach	A	Pkt	3'-5'	3"-4"	½"	40-50	Dislikes warm weather, so plant early.
Swiss Chard	B	Pkt	3'-5'	3"-4"	½"	45-65	Great warm or cool weather crop. Crew cut harvesting keeps plants producing.
Turnip	A	Pkt	3'-5'	4"-6"	¼"	35-60	Plant thickly and enjoy thinnings as greens and small roots.

* A - Hardy. Plant as soon as soil can be worked. 20-40 days before last frost. B - Semi-hardy. Can take some frost. Plant 10-30 days before last frost. C -Tender. Cannot stand frost. Plant on or after average last frost date or protect plants.

MEAN DATE OF LAST 32° TEMPERATURE IN SPRING

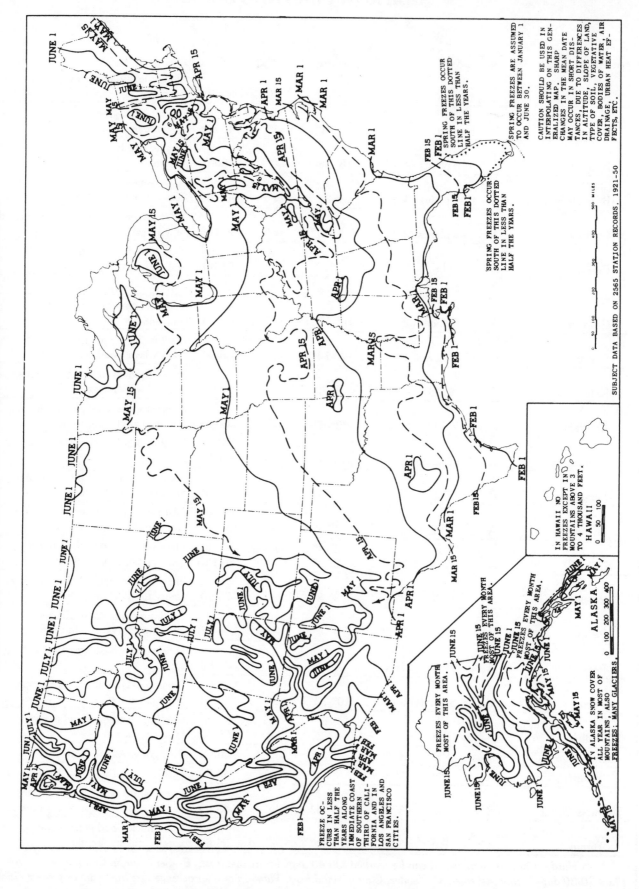

MEAN DATE OF FIRST 32° TEMPERATURE IN AUTUMN

CAUTION SHOULD BE USED IN INTERPOLATING ON THIS GENERALIZED MAP. SHARP CHANGES IN THE MEAN DATE MAY OCCUR IN SHORT DISTANCES, DUE TO DIFFERENCES IN ALTITUDE, SLOPE OF LAND, TYPE OF SOIL, VEGETATIVE COVER, BODIES OF WATER, AIR DRAINAGE, URBAN HEAT EFFECTS, ETC.

AUTUMN (FALL) FREEZES ARE ASSUMED TO OCCUR BETWEEN JULY 1 AND DECEMBER 31.

FALL FREEZES OCCUR SOUTH OF THIS DOTTED LINE IN LESS THAN HALF THE YEARS.

FALL FREEZES OCCUR SOUTH OF THIS DOTTED LINE IN LESS THAN HALF THE YEARS.

SUBJECT DATA BASED ON 2565 STATION RECORDS, 1921-50

FREEZE OC-JAN OCCURS IN LESS THAN HALF THE YEARS ALONG IMMEDIATE COAST OF SOUTHERN CALIFORNIA AND IN LOS ANGELES AND SAN FRANCISCO CITIES.

IN HAWAII NO FREEZES EXCEPT IN MOUNTAINS ABOVE 3 TO 4 THOUSAND FEET.

HAWAII
0   50   100

IN ALASKA SNOW COVER ALL YEAR IN MOST OF MOUNTAINS. ALSO FREEZES: MANY GLACIERS

FREEZES EVERY MONTH MOST OF THIS AREA.

FREEZES EVERY MONTH MOST OF THIS AREA.

FREEZES EVERY MONTH MOST OF THIS AREA.

ALASKA
0 100 200 300 400

29

Give Crops a Boost

Many crops have big appetites, and if they're to produce their best, they need a mid-season snack.

Gardeners call it side-dressing. That's adding fertilizer—commercial or natural—to the soil. It can be done several ways.

Banding. Great with single-row crops like corn. Make a shallow furrow with a hoe six inches to one side of the row. Drop in a thin band of fertilizer, then hoe soil over it.

Circling. Spoon-feed tomatoes, peppers, and other transplanted crops. Use a hoe or trowel to make a circle around each plant six inches away from the stem. Spoon in the fertilizer, just a teaspoon per plant, then cover the fertilizer with soil.

Top-Dressing. For wide rows. Sprinkle natural fertilizers—bone meal, alfalfa meal, compost—over the row. Don't use commercial fertilizers. They will stick to the plants and burn them.

Vegetable	When	Amount of Complete Fertilizer
Broccoli	As heads begin to form	1-2 tablespoons per plant
Brussels Sprouts	When sprouts are size of marbles	1 tablespoon per plant
Cabbage	When heads start to form	1 tablespoon per plant
Cauliflower	When leaves reach maximum size	1-2 tablespoons per plant
Chard	After first harvest	1 tablespoon per foot of 16-inch wide row
Corn	Twice, when ten inches high and when it starts to tassle	1 tablespoon per plant each time
Cucumbers, Melons & Winter Squash	Before vines start to run	1 tablespoon per plant
Eggplant	When blossoms form	1 tablespoon per plant
Leeks	When 8-12 inches tall	2-3 handsful of compost mounded around each plant
Onions	When 6-8 inches tall, and every two weeks after until bulbs start to expand	2-3 cups per 10 feet of wide row
Peppers	Blossom time	1 teaspoon (and no more)
Pole Beans	In South only, a week after first picking, then every 3-4 weeks	1 teaspoon per plant
Potatoes	6-7 weeks after planting	1 tablespoon per plant, before hilling
Summer Squash	When buds form	1-2 tablespoons per plant
Tomatoes	First blossoms	1-2 tablespoons per plant

Instead of one tablespoon of a complete fertilizer such as 5-10-10, you can substitute two handfuls good compost, two handfuls dehydrated manure, or one to two tablespoons alfalfa meal.

Plant Green Manures To Improve Your Soil

For better vegetables and far fewer weeds, raise green manures. These are crops that are raised primarily to improve the soil, and they're turned under at the height of their growth.

Green manures will keep soils from eroding. They'll catch nutrients in the soil that might leach far down into the ground. Best of all, they'll improve the soil—add nutrients, break up clay soils, add organic matter to sandy soils, smother weeds. Try them in unused sections of your garden, and blanket your garden with green manure in the fall.

Here are some to try:

Garden Peas: Harvest the peas, then till under the nitrogen-rich vines. Use one pound per 100 square feet. Inoculate seeds for greater nitrogen-fixing. See page 22.

Beans: Use green or yellow bush varieties. Inoculate seeds. Plant one pound per 100 square feet after last spring frost, harvest them, then till under the vines. Will choke out weeds, meaning fewer weeds next year.

Buckwheat: Sow two to three pounds per 1,000 square feet any time from one to two weeks before last spring frost to five to six weeks before expected first fall frost. Turn crop under in six weeks. If it matures, seed will be scattered, and it will reseed itself, so can be a nuisance. Buckwheat is great for choking out weeds. Good in all regions.

Annual Ryegrass: Plant two to three pounds per 1,000 square feet any time from midsummer up to three weeks before first fall frost. Freezing temperatures kill grass, and it forms a heavy insulating blanket over the soil. Easy to work into soil in the spring; it won't delay spring planting. Good in all regions. Don't plant perennial ryegrass.

Winter Rye: Plant two pounds per 1,000 square feet two to three weeks before the first fall frost. It will grow in fall, resume growth in spring. Till under when it is ten to twelve inches tall. If it grows higher, it will be more difficult to till under, and may delay planting as it decomposes. Good protection against winter erosion.

Beans, Bush and Pole

A favorite gardening crop that's easy to grow, productive, can be grown throughout the United States, and does well in almost any soil but a wet one. Bush beans are an excellent wide-row crop and grow well in narrow rows and on raised beds too. Plant any time from just after the last spring frost to six or seven weeks before the expected first frost. I plant bush beans in super wide rows or blocks because I never seem to have enough of this family favorite. Bush beans grow fifteen to twenty inches tall, pole beans as high as fifteen feet, but harvesting becomes difficult at that altitude, so six to eight feet is much more convenient. Some gardeners prefer pole beans because they can raise more in less space, the harvesting season is longer, and many varieties have a delicious, nut-like flavor.

Planting: For a wide row of bush beans, broadcast beans three to six inches apart. Using a rake, pull up soil from beyond the wide row and cover seeds with a one-inch layer. Tamp the seedbed down gently with the back of a hoe. For narrow rows, sow beans two to four inches apart, covering with an inch of soil, space rows eighteen to twenty-four inches apart, and thin to four to six inches apart. For pole beans, try tying three or four eight-foot poles together at the top, and set them up tepee style. Plant five or six seeds per pole, and thin to four plants. Or set up two poles about eight feet apart, link them at the top and bottom with a wire or rope, then dangle strings down from the wire or rope for the beans to climb. Plant beans about six inches apart. Winds will test the strength of these poles, so make them strong and firmly implanted. In all methods, dust beans with inoculant. See page 22.

Cultivation: Avoid cultivating after rain or when dew is on plants, to keep from spreading disease. Hoe gently, to avoid harming roots. Add mulch when plants are up and soil is warm.

Harvesting: Stay out of the garden when plants are wet. Picking early and often increases the harvest.

Enemies: The Mexican bean beetle, tan with eight black spots on each wing, is larger than a ladybug. Hand pick these beetles, to prevent them from laying egg clusters on undersides of leaves. It is larvae from these eggs that ravage leaves, then eat beans. During harvest, watch for egg clusters and destroy them. Rotenone is also used for beetle control. Select beans resistant to fungus diseases, such as the rusts.

Varieties: Green bush beans include Improved Tendergreen (Fifty-six days to harvest. Meaty, dark green, stringless, mosaic resistant). Tendercrop (Fifty-three days. Smooth round green pods, mosaic resistant). Yellow varieties are Brittle Wax (Fifty-two days. Heavy yields). Pencil Pod Wax (Fifty-four days. Hardy, heavy yielder, good for late fall or early spring plantings). Pole varieties recommended include Kentucky Wonder (Sixty-five days), Blue Lake (Sixty days).

Suggestions: Bush beans are good succession crops to follow peas and early spinach.

A tepee of pole beans is easy to create and a delight to children.

19 _88_

Planting	Variety	Date Planted	Amount Planted (Row Length)
1.		4/25	1-Row
2.			
3.			

Harvest Dates	Variety	Expected	Actual
1.			
2.			
3.			

Satisfied With Variety, Amount?

19 ___

Planting	Variety	Date Planted	Amount Planted (Row Length)
1.			
2.			
3.			

Harvest Dates	Variety	Expected	Actual
1.			
2.			
3.			

Satisfied With Variety, Amount?

19 ___

Planting	Variety	Date Planted	Amount Planted (Row Length)
1.			
2.			
3.			

Harvest Dates	Variety	Expected	Actual
1.			
2.			
3.			

Satisfied With Variety, Amount?

19 ____

Planting	Variety	Date Planted	Amount Planted (Row Length)
1.			
2.			
3.			

Harvest Dates	Variety	Expected	Actual
1.			
2.			
3.			

Satisfied With Variety, Amount?

19 ____

Planting	Variety	Date Planted	Amount Planted (Row Length)
1.			
2.			
3.			

Harvest Dates	Variety	Expected	Actual
1.			
2.			
3.			

Satisfied With Variety, Amount?

19 ____

Planting	Variety	Date Planted	Amount Planted (Row Length)
1.			
2.			
3.			

Harvest Dates	Variety	Expected	Actual
1.			
2.			
3.			

Satisfied With Variety, Amount?

Beans, Shell, Bush and Pole

Grown for shelling from pods, then eaten green, or allowed to dry on the vine before shelling. There are dozens of varieties, many native to the United States and dating back to its earliest history, when many depended so much on beans as a source of protein. These and other bean types are doubly valuable to the gardener since they enrich the soil with nitrogen. Beans are good to plant where some "hungry" crop, such as corn, grew the previous year. Four ounces of seed will yield eight pounds of shelled beans. Bush shell beans are great for wide rows and raised beds, where four ounces will seed ten to fifteen feet.

Planting: See page 32 under Bush and Pole Beans.

Cultivation: Avoid contact with plants when they are wet, to avoid spreading disease. Beans are shallow-rooted, so weeds should be scraped away, carefully. Mulch is helpful, particularly in dry periods. Side-dressing isn't necessary.

Harvesting: Shell beans are left on the plants until the pods are mature and the beans push out in the pods. Shell beans for immediate eating (or freezing or canning) should be picked when beans can be seen in the pods, but before the pod has passed the growth stage and begun to dry. For dry beans, pods can be allowed to dry on the plant, or mature plants can be cut and stacked to dry, then beans picked off them.

Enemies: See listing under Bush and Pole Beans, page 32.

Varieties: The hundreds of varieties of beans make selection an adventure. Choose beans popular in your area, since they must grow well there, and try several varieties each year until you find your favorite. Save seeds; cross pollination is not a problem.

French Horticulture (Sixty-eight days to harvest. Good producer) and Red Kidney (Ninety-five days. Large beans) are good in the three stages of growth. Try them first as snap beans, then green shell beans, then dry beans. The large Red Kidneys are particularly versatile, baked, boiled, or in soups. They're delicious. In the South, favorites are Southern or Crowder peas (they are beans). They can be grown wherever lima beans do well.

Suggestions: Dried beans are easiest to shell when pods are so dry they're brittle. If you have a lot, put a load of beans in a burlap bag, tie it up, and have children jump on it. Then shake the beans to the top of the bag. If you're careful, you can pour out most of the beans and few of the broken pods. Pour them out on a blanket on a windy day, and most of the chaff will be blown away. Sort and store dried beans in a capped glass jar and keep in a cool place.

Let pods get brittle-dry before attempting to shell them.

Beans, Lima, Pole and Bush

These are the fussiest beans to grow—and they're well worth the effort. Home grown limas are far tastier than the limas you buy, either fresh or frozen. Limas do best where summers are long and hot, and night temperatures remain above 50° for two months. Can be eaten green or dried. Limas need fertile, well-drained, mellow soil and do poorly on heavy clays. Add compost if you have it. Half-pound of bush seeds can yield twenty-five pounds of pods. Fine for wide rows and really appreciate the extra heat provided by raised beds.

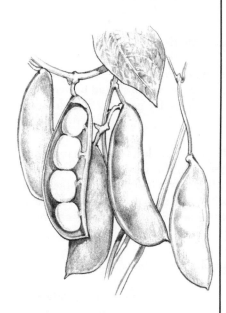

Planting: Dust seed with pea and bean inoculant. Plant lima beans week or more after the day of the average last spring frost, when soil has warmed to at least 65°. Seed planted too early will rot. In wide rows, plant bush seed six to eight inches apart. Cover with light soil. For narrow row, plant bush beans four to six inches apart, one inch deep in rows twenty-four to thirty inches apart. For pole beans, see instructions on page 32, Bush and Pole Beans.

Cultivation: Avoid contact with wet plants. Beans are shallow-rooted, so do not cultivate deeply. Limas need a lot of water. Water early in the day, so leaves can dry. A single heavy watering, to get the water down six inches into the soil, is far better than daily sprinkling.

Harvesting: Pick vines clean to promote bearing. Pods are ready for picking when beans have reached full size but pods have not yet turned yellow. Try one meal of beans that haven't reached mature size, for a tasy treat. Harvest at the green stage for shell beans, or allow to dry. Limas are difficult to shell.

Enemies: If weather is cool and wet at harvest time, downy mildew may cover pods with white patches. Burn these vines.

Varieties: Limas, called butter beans in the South, are small-seeded and large-seeded, and different varieties are popular in different areas. Among bush beans, Fordhook 242 (Seventy-five days to harvest. Large beans. Heat resistant) is popular for main crop. In South, Henderson (Sixty-five days. Small seed) is old standby. In North, Dixie Butterpea (Seventy-five days. Small seeded, heavy crop) is popular. For pole beans, King of the Garden (Eighty-eight days. Heavy producer) is one of the best.

Suggestions: If you live where getting a crop of limas is a problem because of the cold climate, here are things to try:
   1. I planted a twenty-foot row of bush limas, half under a plastic tunnel, the remainder unprotected. The difference was incredible. The protected beans were up and producing much earlier, and had a much heavier set of beans.
   2. Plant sparsely in wide rows on a raised bed. A raised bed can be five to ten degrees warmer than the surrounding soil, and limas like that extra heat.

19 _____

Planting	Variety	Date Planted	Amount Planted (Row Length)
1. _____		_____	_____
2. _____		_____	_____
3. _____		_____	_____

Harvest Dates	Variety	Expected	Actual
1. _____		_____	_____
2. _____		_____	_____
3. _____		_____	_____

Satisfied With Variety, Amount? _____

_____

19 _____

Planting	Variety	Date Planted	Amount Planted (Row Length)
1. _____		_____	_____
2. _____		_____	_____
3. _____		_____	_____

Harvest Dates	Variety	Expected	Actual
1. _____		_____	_____
2. _____		_____	_____
3. _____		_____	_____

Satisfied With Variety, Amount? _____

_____

19 _____

Planting	Variety	Date Planted	Amount Planted (Row Length)
1. _____		_____	_____
2. _____		_____	_____
3. _____		_____	_____

Harvest Dates	Variety	Expected	Actual
1. _____		_____	_____
2. _____		_____	_____
3. _____		_____	_____

Satisfied With Variety, Amount? _____

_____

19 ____

Planting	Variety	Date Planted	Amount Planted (Row Length)
1.			
2.			
3.			

Harvest Dates	Variety	Expected	Actual
1.			
2.			
3.			

Satisfied With Variety, Amount?

19 ____

Planting	Variety	Date Planted	Amount Planted (Row Length)
1.			
2.			
3.			

Harvest Dates	Variety	Expected	Actual
1.			
2.			
3.			

Satisfied With Variety, Amount?

19 ____

Planting	Variety	Date Planted	Amount Planted (Row Length)
1.			
2.			
3.			

Harvest Dates	Variety	Expected	Actual
1.			
2.			
3.			

Satisfied With Variety, Amount?

Beets

Raised throughout the United States. Cold-hardy and easy to grow. Resistant to insects and diseases. Prefer sunny, sandy loam, with compost well dug in. Small roots and early greens are a delicious treat. Fall crop easy to store. Half-ounce of seed will yield about fifty pounds; a packet of seed will stretch only along two to three feet of wide row. A good crop for wide rows and raised beds.

Planting: A beet "seed" is really a beet "fruit" consisting of three or four seeds, so seedlings often are in clumps. Sow sparsely, two to four inches apart in wide row, one to two inches apart in narrow rows, four weeks before last spring frost, or as early as soil can be worked. Space narrow rows twelve to eighteen inches apart. Cover seeds with half-inch of soil. If seedlings are too thick in wide or narrow row, drag teeth of iron rake across row. It will thin effectively, and ragged looking bed will quickly revive. When plants are six inches tall, thin again, to keep individual beets four inches apart. This time use thinnings for tasty greens. Mulch seedlings in single row. Start successive plantings two to three weeks apart for continuing supply. For fall and storage crop, plant six to eight weeks before the first fall frost.

Harvesting: Harvesting begins with thinnings when roots are less than one inch in diameter and the beets are at their sweet, tender best. Beets become woody if left in ground after maturity. If growing in a wide row, keep picking the earliest beets, giving the remainder space to grow. When harvesting for storage, leave a half-inch of stems attached to avoid bleeding. For winter storage, plant late, leave beets in ground until after first light frost, then store in cold (35°-40°), with high humidity. Try storing them in plastic bags that have ventilation holes. Beets are easily canned or frozen, and a real treat when pickled. In the South, gardeners can cover a row of late beets with a foot of mulch, then dig up the beets when wanted. This works in the North, too, if winters are mild.

Varieties: For an early crop, try Early Wonder (Fifty-five days to harvest, flattened, globe shaped) and Crosby's Egyptian (Fifty-six days, dark red, tasty). For later crop and fall planting for storage, Detroit Dark Red (Sixty days, dark red and sweet). Lutz Green Leaf (Eighty days) is a big beet that can be eaten either large or small, and is a good keeper. This one has luscious greens—a lot like chard.

Suggestions: Try a variety of golden beets. Many—and I'm among them—prefer their sweet, mild flavor and smooth, tender texture. Some children who "hate beets" will eat these and love them.

When storing beets, leave a half-inch of stems so beets won't bleed.

Broccoli

For a tasty vegetable that's as loaded with as much goodness as a multi-vitamin pill, grow broccoli. It's a fine source of vitamins A, B, and C, and can be grown throughout the United States. It requires a loose, rich soil that will hold moisture. Broccoli likes to mature in cool weather, so aim for an early summer crop, and a fall crop, and forget mid-summer, when broccoli quickly blossoms.

Planting: For the best broccoli, start seeds so that you can get the plants outside in five weeks. Many let the plants get much bigger, and the results are slow production and button size heads. Broccoli is hardy, so can be moved outside before the last frost of the spring. In a wide row, place the plants sixteen inches apart in a 2-1-2 pattern. For a fall crop (and many believe the fall crop is better), start plants ten to twelve weeks before the first fall frost.

Cultivation: Broccoli is shallow-rooted, so cultivate carefully, to avoid damage to roots. Mulch to preserve moisture, since plants need continuing supply. Sidedress with a high-nitrogen fertilizer, about fifteen days after plants are set out, then again when heads begin to form.

Harvesting: Broccoli is grown for its flower-bud clusters, and the tender stems near them. Cut clusters with a four- to six-inch stalk before buds open. After that head is cut, small clusters will form in the leaf axils, and these, too, may be harvested. Broccoli freezes well.

Enemies: If the danger of eating cabbage worms has kept you from growing this vegetable, try it again, and spray or dust with Bacillus thuringiensis, sold as Dipel, Thuricide, and Biotrol. It's a naturally occurring bacterium that's harmless to all but the worms. I start spraying when the first white butterflies flutter into my garden, and keep spraying every seven to ten days until the end of the harvest. It's wonderful—it eliminates the problem, and makes eating broccoli a joy instead of a constant search for those crawly little strangers.

Varieties: Premium Crop (Sixty days from time of transplant to harvest. Deep blue-green. Disease resistant. Good fresh or frozen). Green Comet (Fifty days. A deep blue-green. Holds shape well).

Suggestions: To avoid disease problems, don't plant broccoli or any other cabbage family member in the same place more than once every four years. Keep cutting side shoots, and plants will keep producing. The fall broccoli crop often requires less spraying.

Pick off lower leaves of transplants to give plants a faster start.

19 ____

Planting	Variety	Date Planted	Amount Planted (Row Length)
1.			
2.			
3.			

Harvest Dates	Variety	Expected	Actual
1.			
2.			
3.			

Satisfied With Variety, Amount?

19 ____

Planting	Variety	Date Planted	Amount Planted (Row Length)
1.			
2.			
3.			

Harvest Dates	Variety	Expected	Actual
1.			
2.			
3.			

Satisfied With Variety, Amount?

19 ____

Planting	Variety	Date Planted	Amount Planted (Row Length)
1.			
2.			
3.			

Harvest Dates	Variety	Expected	Actual
1.			
2.			
3.			

Satisfied With Variety, Amount?

19 ___

Planting	Variety	Date Planted	Amount Planted (Row Length)
1.			
2.			
3.			

Harvest Dates	Variety	Expected	Actual
1.			
2.			
3.			

Satisfied With Variety, Amount?

_____

_____

19 ___

Planting	Variety	Date Planted	Amount Planted (Row Length)
1.			
2.			
3.			

Harvest Dates	Variety	Expected	Actual
1.			
2.			
3.			

Satisfied With Variety, Amount?

_____

_____

19 ___

Planting	Variety	Date Planted	Amount Planted (Row Length)
1.			
2.			
3.			

Harvest Dates	Variety	Expected	Actual
1.			
2.			
3.			

Satisfied With Variety, Amount?

_____

_____

Brussels Sprouts

Easy to raise throughout the United States. When other vegetables are killed by the first fall frosts, Brussels sprouts are only improved. Aim for a late fall crop, and pick long after the first snowfall. Because of their hardiness, Brussels sprouts are almost a perennial in the South, where the sprouts can be collected throughout the winter. This vegetable is disliked by many who have only tasted summer sprouts, or overcooked sprouts, both of which taste like very strong cabbage.

Planting: Plan on a mid-fall harvest and allow thirty to forty-five days from seed to transplants, and seventy-five days from transplant to harvest. In Vermont, I sow seeds in a small area in the garden about June 1. A month later, I transplant them into wide rows, and my crop begins to be ready in mid-September. Count on twenty-five plants in a fifty-foot row yielding more than twenty-five pounds of sprouts. Plant in a staggered formation in a wide row, placing plants sixteen to eighteen inches apart.

Cultivation: Need lots of moisture, so mulch heavily. Because roots are near surface, don't hoe deeply.

Harvesting: If you miscalculate and raise summer sprouts, harvest them when they're tiny, and you can enjoy them. In fall, as your correctly timed plants have their first sprouts, break off the lower leaves, to allow more room for sprouts. As you harvest, continue to take off leaves, stimulating plant to grow taller and produce more. Brussels sprouts taste best after being nipped by frost.

Enemies: See under Enemies, Broccoli, for the sure way to rid your cole crops of cabbage worms. To avoid disease problems, don't plant Brussels sprouts, or any other members of the cabbage family, in same area more than once every four years.

Varieties: Jade Cross (Eighty days from time of transplant to harvest. Uniform, firm sprouts. Disease-resistant). Long Island Improved (Ninety days. Tight heads).

Suggestions: One of the finest ways to enjoy Brussels sprouts is to pick a batch of the smallest ones, early in the season, and add them to tossed salads or coleslaw. When cooking sprouts, cut an X with a knife in the bottom of each sprout. This insures even cooking.

Cabbage

Giant cabbages win the blue ribbons at the county fair, but smaller ones make more sense in the kitchen, where a five-pound head is about right for a single meal. That's why I urge you to plant cabbages closer together than the seed packets and other books advise. You'll get smaller heads, but more of them in the same amount of space.

Planting: Start transplants inside four to six weeks before date of expected last frost. Harden off, then plant outside as much as two weeks before the frost date. In twenty-inch wide row, set in 3-2-3 formation, in sixteen-inch row, set in 2-1-2 formation, with plants ten to twelve inches apart. In narrow rows, set plants ten to twelve inches apart. Plant in rich, moist soil, with compost added. If cutworms are a problem, wrap each stem with a two-inch square of newspaper.

Cultivation: Cabbages are very shallow rooted, so pull weeds under plants. and hoe only the top half-inch of soil around the plants. But planted in wide rows, there's little problem with weeds. If cabbages show signs of cracking, twist the head to break some of the roots and thus slow the growing pace.

Harvesting: For a long season of eating enjoyment, begin harvesting when cabbages reach softball size. In fall, cabbages are improved by light frost, but should be stored before heavy frosts. Cabbage can be stored in a cool cellar for as much as two months. Bring them in as late as possible, and wrap them in newspapers.

Enemies: The white butterfly, so innocent looking in its flight around cabbage plants, is the worst enemy, since it signals the impending arrival of the cabbage worm. I've known people to use tennis racquets to down the butterflies. Better approach is the use of Bacillus thuringiensis, described under Broccoli Enemies. Red varieties of cabbages have fewer cabbage worm problems.

Varieties: Early: Stonehead (Sixty-seven days from transplant to maturity. Four-pound heads). Emerald Cross (Sixty-four days, four- to five-pound heads). Golden Acre (Sixty-four days, four- to five-pound heads). Early Round Dutch (Seventy-one days, firm and round, and slow to split, with four- to five-pound heads). Midseason: Burpee's Copenhagen Market (Seventy-two days. Four- to five-pound heads). Late: Danish Ballhead (105 days, round, very firm heads). Eastern Ballhead (Ninety-five days, six- to seven-pound heads). Red Cabbage: (very worth trying). Ruby Ball (Sixty-eight days, extra early, firm, round, dark red heads). Resistant Red Acre (Seventy-six days. Deep red, good for early yield). Savoy: Savoy King (Ninety days. Good fall crop with four- to five-pound heads).

Suggestions: The most common way to cook cabbage—boiling—is the worst way. It destroys nutrients and ruins the flavor. Janet Ballantyne, author of The Joy of Gardening Cookbook, suggests three alternatives: steaming for five to eight minutes, blanching for four to eight minutes, or sauteing, or stir frying, in oil, not butter, for three to five minutes.

If cabbages grow too fast, the top of heads may split open.

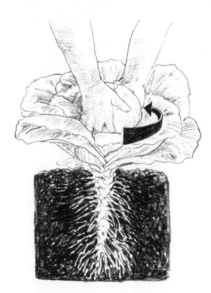

At first sign of this, give head a twist, half way around. This breaks off some roots, and slows growth.

19 ____

Planting	Variety	Date Planted	Amount Planted (Row Length)
1.			
2.			
3.			

Harvest Dates	Variety	Expected	Actual
1.			
2.			
3.			

Satisfied With Variety, Amount?

19 ____

Planting	Variety	Date Planted	Amount Planted (Row Length)
1.			
2.			
3.			

Harvest Dates	Variety	Expected	Actual
1.			
2.			
3.			

Satisfied With Variety, Amount?

19 ____

Planting	Variety	Date Planted	Amount Planted (Row Length)
1.			
2.			
3.			

Harvest Dates	Variety	Expected	Actual
1.			
2.			
3.			

Satisfied With Variety, Amount?

19 ____

Planting	Variety	Date Planted	Amount Planted (Row Length)
1.			
2.			
3.			

Harvest Dates	Variety	Expected	Actual
1.			
2.			
3.			

Satisfied With Variety, Amount?

_____

19 ____

Planting	Variety	Date Planted	Amount Planted (Row Length)
1.			
2.			
3.			

Harvest Dates	Variety	Expected	Actual
1.			
2.			
3.			

Satisfied With Variety, Amount?

_____

19 ____

Planting	Variety	Date Planted	Amount Planted (Row Length)
1.			
2.			
3.			

Harvest Dates	Variety	Expected	Actual
1.			
2.			
3.			

Satisfied With Variety, Amount?

_____

Carrots

America's favorite root crop, and a great wide-row crop. In the South, carrots are grown in the fall, winter, and spring. In the North, they're a summer crop. Because carrots are used in so many ways—in salads, soups, stews, and other dishes—it's difficult to raise too many. Small carrots, rarely found in the supermarket, are most useful in the kitchen, and freeze well. Carrots grow best in rich, mellow, deeply worked soil, so are ideal for raised beds. Fresh manure makes carrots grow hairy roots, so don't use.

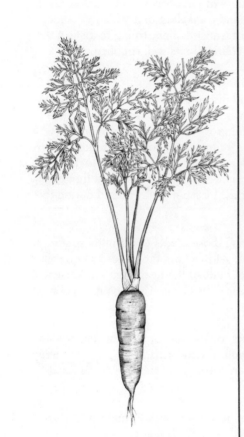

Planting: I use an empty garlic powder bottle to sow carrot seeds. This is an easy way to scatter them evenly over a wide row. Cover with a quarter-inch of fine soil. If I've sown too thickly, I pull a steel rake about a half to three-quarters of an inch into the soil, across the row once. This thins the planting and removes many of the weeds that are just emerging.

Cultivating: I like to sow a few icicle radishes in the row. They come up quickly, provide an early harvest, and cultivate within the row when they're removed. Carrots planted in a wide row quickly blanket the row, and discourage most weeds.

Harvesting: My second thinning begins the harvest, since I wait until the carrots are finger-thick, then thin them to eat. This thinning gives the remaining plants space to grow, since those that are left are two inches apart.

Enemies: Usually free of enemies. If tiny holes are found in the root, it is the work of the larvae of the carrot rust fly. Avoid planting where celery or carrots were grown previously, and sprinkle wood ashes in the row. If the problem is a continuing one, avoid planting an early crop for one year. A crop planted after June 1 will avoid the larvae cycle of this fly.

Varieties: Long, slim varieties should be grown in deep, loose, sandy soil, chunky ones are great in heavier soils. Chantenay Long (Sixty days to maturity. Long and tapered). Short n' Sweet (Sixty-eight days. Will grow in heavy soil). Danvers 126 (Sixty-five days. My favorite, and one of the tastiest varieties).

Suggestions: Here are several ways to store carrots. 1. In the garden, heavily mulching the top and sides of the row with at least a foot of hay or leaves. Mulch heavily or they'll lose their crunch; eat soon after digging or they'll spoil. 2. In the refrigerator, if you have room. They'll keep for several months in plastic bags. 3. In a box, in a cool room. Dig the carrots, let them dry for an hour in the sun, snip off the tops. Place a four-inch layer of dampened peat moss in the bottom of a big box. Put in a single layer of carrots, keeping them two inches from the sides of the box. Cover with a half-inch layer of dampened peat moss, then fill the box, alternating layers of peat moss and carrots. Top with six inches of peat moss. 4. Place in plastic garbage bags in which holes have been punched. Store in a cool root cellar, or a basement, closet, or garage.

Cauliflower

If you've had trouble raising cauliflower, as I've had, try the method that works well for me—raise cauliflower as a fall crop. This fussiest member of the cabbage family requires a deep, rich loam, an abundance of organic material in the soil, cool temperatures, lots of moisture, ample fertilizer—and a little luck to raise a good crop. Set twenty-five plants in a fifty-foot single row, or plant in a 3-2-3 formation in a twenty-inch wide row, with plants ten to twelve inches apart.

Planting: To grow as a fall crop, I want to harvest these plants as close as I can to my expected first fall frost date of October 3, so I plant seeds in a small part of the garden in mid-June and transplant to a wide row about five or six weeks later. I'm careful about transplanting, trying to disturb the roots as little as possible, and keeping young plants well supplied with water.

Cultivation: I cultivate lightly to avoid disrupting those shallow roots. A heavy mulch around the plants conserves moisture and tends to keep the soil cooler; the plants respond with good growth. When the cauliflower heads are about 2 inches in diameter, it's time to blanch them to keep them sweet and white. I do this by bending leaves over the head, and tucking them in on the other side until the head is well hidden. I've found that cauliflower is ready to eat 4-10 days after this. I keep it well watered during this final stage.

Harvesting: If you've managed to bring those plants to a fruitful maturity, don't spoil it all by delaying the harvest. At this time the heads may be six to twelve inches across. If the individual buds of the head begin to loosen, the head is called "ricey," and it has passed its prime. Consign it to your compost pile.

Enemies: Cabbage worms will dine on cauliflower. Spoil their dinner with the method used under Enemies, Broccoli. If cutworms are a problem, wrap the stem of each transplant with a two-inch square of newspaper as a cutworm collar.

Varieties: Early Snowball (Sixty days from transplant to maturity). Burpeeana (Fifty-eight days. Super Snowball variety. Dependable).

Suggestions: If cauliflower is difficult for you to grow, try a fall crop when it's easier to deal with the crop's dislike of heat. You can keep the soil moist, the weeds down, the soil mulched, and the cauliflower growing without interruption. Slow, steady growth is the key to sweet, tender cauliflower.

19 ____

Planting	Variety	Date Planted	Amount Planted (Row Length)
1.			
2.			
3.			

Harvest Dates	Variety	Expected	Actual
1.			
2.			
3.			

Satisfied With Variety, Amount?

19 ____

Planting	Variety	Date Planted	Amount Planted (Row Length)
1.			
2.			
3.			

Harvest Dates	Variety	Expected	Actual
1.			
2.			
3.			

Satisfied With Variety, Amount?

19 ____

Planting	Variety	Date Planted	Amount Planted (Row Length)
1.			
2.			
3.			

Harvest Dates	Variety	Expected	Actual
1.			
2.			
3.			

Satisfied With Variety, Amount?

19 _____

Planting   Variety   Date Planted   Amount Planted (Row Length)

1. _____   _____   _____

2. _____   _____   _____

3. _____   _____   _____

Harvest Dates   Variety   Expected   Actual

1. _____   _____   _____

2. _____   _____   _____

3. _____   _____   _____

Satisfied With Variety, Amount? _____

_____

19 _____

Planting   Variety   Date Planted   Amount Planted (Row Length)

1. _____   _____   _____

2. _____   _____   _____

3. _____   _____   _____

Harvest Dates   Variety   Expected   Actual

1. _____   _____   _____

2. _____   _____   _____

3. _____   _____   _____

Satisfied With Variety, Amount? _____

_____

19 _____

Planting   Variety   Date Planted   Amount Planted (Row Length)

1. _____   _____   _____

2. _____   _____   _____

3. _____   _____   _____

Harvest Dates   Variety   Expected   Actual

1. _____   _____   _____

2. _____   _____   _____

3. _____   _____   _____

Satisfied With Variety, Amount? _____

_____

Celery

Celery isn't hard to grow. The trick is to grow celery that isn't so strongly celery-ish that it is only fit for flavoring soups, stews, and sauces. Widely dependable, it's grown as a winter crop in the deep South, early spring or late fall crop further north, and as a late summer crop in the North. Rich, moist soil should be prepared with a quantity of rotted manure or compost worked into the growing area. Figure on 100 plants per fifty-foot single row, or a few more in two trenches in a twenty-five foot wide row or on top of a raised bed.

Planting: Soak seeds overnight to speed germination. Start plants indoors ten to twelve weeks before the last spring frost, giving them lots of room in a flat, or transplanting once indoors. About two weeks after the last frost, dig a trench six inches deep, and plant the transplants in the bottom of the trench ten inches apart, set a half-inch deeper than they were. As plants grow, fill in the trench with sandy soil. Celery can be raised in two trenches stretched along a wide row or raised bed.

Cultivation: To keep celery from getting stringy and far too strong, keep it evenly moist, well fed, and blanched. A side-dressing will help, as will extra water in the trench whenever a dry spell threatens. The plants have short, shallow roots, so both moisture and food must be easily available to the plants. I've tried many blanching systems, such as boards and milk cartons. The easiest way I've found is to bank the plants with a sandy soil. The soil can be pulled up as high as the foliage. Washing off that soil after harvesting is not a problem. Separating the stalks and washing them with a brush under running water does it quickly.

Harvesting: It's possible, as the celery grows, to dig down and pick some of the outer stalks. The plant will continue to grow and expand. Later it is easier to harvest the entire plant.

Varieties: Giant Pascal (135 days from date plants are placed in garden). Fordhook (130 days. Good for fall, winter storage). Tendercrisp (100 days. Good for short-season areas).

Suggestions: Celery can be stored for a short time. Leave it in the garden, banking soil up over the plants, and cover it with a layer of straw or hay. It will be fine for one or two months. Or dig up the plants, roots, soil, and all, and place them in a cold frame or in a box of dirt in a root cellar. Keep them moist and they will stay healthy for several months.

Chinese Cabbage

Be prepared for some confusion in names if you grow this cabbage that tastes more like celery and can be used like lettuce. There are two popular varieties, the taller Michihli and the shorter Wong Bok. Both are called Pe Tsai in China and Hakusai in Japan. And don't confuse these with Chinese Mustard Cabbage, or Bok Choy, with its white ribs. A million or more Chinese gardeners may argue against me, but I find it best to raise this vegetable as a fall crop in the North, a winter crop in the South, despite the fact that many seed companies have varieties recommended for spring, and say to plant it then much as you plant lettuce. Chinese cabbage forms a tight, compact head on maturity, and is delicious in coleslaw, stir-fried, or as lettuce in salads. A quarter-ounce of seeds will produce forty heads. Can be grown in wide rows.

Planting: I've discovered several peculiarities about growing Chinese cabbage. One is that if it's grown in the spring it will go to seed quickly and never head, if the weather is too cool—or too hot. Second, it doesn't do well if it's crowded. I found this out through failures, and now know to keep the plants at least eight inches apart. I sprinkle the seeds sparsely in a wide row, and cover with an inch of soil. When the tiny plants come up, I thin them first with a rake, and thin mercilessly until each plant has at least eight inches of elbow room. I plant the seeds seventy-five to eighty days before the first fall frost is expected. In the South, you can start planting a month before the first cool weather of fall, and continue until seventy-five to eighty days before the hot days of early summer.

Cultivation: Keep the plants well watered at all times. The soil should be rich, and side-dressing will stimulate growth. Mulching, too, helps to maintain moisture.

Harvesting: As heads mature, getting firm and fully developed, harvest them. Remove any tough outer leaves. Harvest all before a heavy frost, but don't worry about light frosts because the plants can tolerate them. Chinese cabbage stores surprising well, better than most regular cabbages. They'll keep for up to three months in a cool cellar.

Enemies: Few insects or diseases trouble this hardy immigrant from the East. If cabbage butterflies show interest, spray with Dipel, as described under Enemies, Broccoli.

Varieties: Michihli (Seventy days to harvest. Distinctive, pleasing flavor).

Suggestions: Chinese cabbage will keep for several weeks in the refrigerator. If it looks wilted, revive it with a thirty-minute bath in ice water.

For milder tasting Chinese cabbage, blanch by removing ends of half-gallon milk cartons and placing them over the Chinese cabbage.

19 ____

Planting	Variety	Date Planted	Amount Planted (Row Length)
1.			
2.			
3.			

Harvest Dates	Variety	Expected	Actual
1.			
2.			
3.			

Satisfied With Variety, Amount?

19 ____

Planting	Variety	Date Planted	Amount Planted (Row Length)
1.			
2.			
3.			

Harvest Dates	Variety	Expected	Actual
1.			
2.			
3.			

Satisfied With Variety, Amount?

19 ____

Planting	Variety	Date Planted	Amount Planted (Row Length)
1.			
2.			
3.			

Harvest Dates	Variety	Expected	Actual
1.			
2.			
3.			

Satisfied With Variety, Amount?

19 _____

Planting	Variety	Date Planted	Amount Planted (Row Length)
1. _____		_____	_____
2. _____		_____	_____
3. _____		_____	_____

Harvest Dates	Variety	Expected	Actual
1. _____		_____	_____
2. _____		_____	_____
3. _____		_____	_____

Satisfied With Variety, Amount? _____

_____

19 _____

Planting	Variety	Date Planted	Amount Planted (Row Length)
1. _____		_____	_____
2. _____		_____	_____
3. _____		_____	_____

Harvest Dates	Variety	Expected	Actual
1. _____		_____	_____
2. _____		_____	_____
3. _____		_____	_____

Satisfied With Variety, Amount? _____

_____

19 _____

Planting	Variety	Date Planted	Amount Planted (Row Length)
1. _____		_____	_____
2. _____		_____	_____
3. _____		_____	_____

Harvest Dates	Variety	Expected	Actual
1. _____		_____	_____
2. _____		_____	_____
3. _____		_____	_____

Satisfied With Variety, Amount? _____

_____

Collards

I'm one Yankee who has grown to love this botanical symbol of the Old South; Southerners know a good vegetable with few growing problems. More Northerners should try growing collards. They'll take cold weather, and warm weather that would do a cabbage in. Their flavor is excellent, with just a hint of their close relative, the cabbage, and they can be cooked and served in the many ways that greens can be prepared. They're rich in vitamins A and C.

Planting: In North, when ground can be worked, and in South, either in spring or in fall, plant seeds thinly and a half-inch deep, in rows three feet apart. Or plant in wide rows, thinning so plants are ten to twelve inches apart. In rows, these four-foot plants are usually kept two feet apart. Or plant seeds in the North in mid-July, for a fall crop. A frost only enhances their flavor.

Cultivation: Strive for rapid growth by working compost or manure into seedbed, and by mulching crop. Shallow cultivation is advised to avoid cutting roots.

Harvesting: Pick the smaller leaves while fresh and bright green. They have smaller midribs, and so are more tender. Do not pick or damage the central bud, or growth of the plant will be halted.

Enemies: The cabbage worm, of course. See Enemies, Broccoli, for halting this fellow in his tracks. Scatter wood ashes around base of plants to discourage root maggots. Avoid planting this or any other members of the cabbage family in the same location more than once every four years.

Varieties: Georgia (Eighty days to harvesting. Mild). Vates (Eighty days. More compact).

Suggestions: Cooks introduced to collards often find them coarse and somewhat strong in flavor. The home gardener can overcome this difficulty by picking the youngest, greenest, and most tender of the leaves. Collards are usually finely chopped, boiled in salted water until just tender, then served with butter or bacon fat and seasonings. Or they can be boiled, then sprinkled with butter and a sharp grated cheese and cooked just until the cheese melts. A Southern recipe is to shred six cups of raw leaves, boil them in salted water, drain them, then mix with six tablespoons of diced lean salt pork, and season with salt and pepper. Don't overcook collards. They should be limp, but not mushy.

Corn

One of the best reasons for having a home garden. Corn needs a lot of space and, being a hungry crop, requires a fertile, warm, well-drained but moist soil. Good gardeners insure a supply that lasts for weeks by planting varieties that mature on different dates, with the latest varieties usually the tastiest.

Planting: Plant each variety in short blocks, at least four rows wide, rather than single long rows, for better pollination. Make furrows with hoe, one to two inches deep and thirty inches apart. If space is a problem, plant double rows ten inches apart, with thirty inches between the double rows. If drainage is a problem, plant double rows on raised beds. Sow seeds four to five inches apart. Pat in place with back of hoe, pull soil over seeds, then firm with back of hoe. Once up, thin plants to eight to ten inches apart.

Cultivating: Keep young plants free of weeds by hoeing, and remember roots are very shallow. Hill every two weeks, pulling soil up around plants. This anchors corn in a windstorm and buries the weeds. Side-dress when corn is knee high and again when it tassels. With a hoe, make a shallow furrow six inches from the plants, sprinkle in a thin line of fertilizer, about one tablespoon of 10-10-10 per plant, and cover with soil.

Harvesting: The common advice is to have the water boiling before you pick the corn. Equally important is to pick corn when it has reached proper development. Ears too immature to eat have small kernels with watery juice. Next is the eating stage, the milk stage when the kernels become plump and sweet. Finally the dough stage, when sugars have turned to starch, and corn is unfit to eat. Pick when silks first become brown and ends of ears feel blunt, not pointed.

Enemies: Plant seeds treated with fungicide to avoid damping off, especially in cool, moist soil. If birds are a problem, buy one-inch mesh chicken wire, twelve inches wide. Partially fold it in center, then place this tent over the row. Raccoons are masters at detecting exactly when corn is ready. Before they attack, spread moth crystals at end of rows and along outer rows. Coons dislike the taste of them. Or try one of the other 101 ways to discourage coons. An electric fence, carefully placed, is one of the best.

Varieties: Experiment to match your growing conditions and your tastes to the best varieties. Sugar and Gold (Sixty-seven days, tender, sweet kernels. Great for short seasons). Butter and Sugar (Seventy-three days. Favorite hybrid with its delicious white and yellow kernels). Silver Queen (Ninety-two days. Hybrid. In my opinion, the tops for eating). Yellow variety, Golden Bantam (Eighty days. Open pollinated. An old favorite, and deservedly so).

Suggestions: If wind knocking down your corn is a problem, try digging a six-inch trench with a hoe, planting in it, then filling trench as corn grows. Later, hill, as described above. Or, far easier, plant the stockier varieties.

Country Gentleman

Country Gentleman is an old variety of corn, not a hybrid, and the kernels are scattered along the ear, not in neat rows. But—and this is why you raise corn—it's delicious. Try it.

19 ____

Planting	Variety	Date Planted	Amount Planted (Row Length)
1.			
2.			
3.			

Harvest Dates	Variety	Expected	Actual
1.			
2.			
3.			

Satisfied With Variety, Amount?

19 ____

Planting	Variety	Date Planted	Amount Planted (Row Length)
1.			
2.			
3.			

Harvest Dates	Variety	Expected	Actual
1.			
2.			
3.			

Satisfied With Variety, Amount?

19 ____

Planting	Variety	Date Planted	Amount Planted (Row Length)
1.			
2.			
3.			

Harvest Dates	Variety	Expected	Actual
1.			
2.			
3.			

Satisfied With Variety, Amount?

19 ____

Planting	Variety	Date Planted	Amount Planted (Row Length)
1.			
2.			
3.			

Harvest Dates	Variety	Expected	Actual
1.			
2.			
3.			

Satisfied With Variety, Amount?

19 ____

Planting	Variety	Date Planted	Amount Planted (Row Length)
1.			
2.			
3.			

Harvest Dates	Variety	Expected	Actual
1.			
2.			
3.			

Satisfied With Variety, Amount?

19 ____

Planting	Variety	Date Planted	Amount Planted (Row Length)
1.			
2.			
3.			

Harvest Dates	Variety	Expected	Actual
1.			
2.			
3.			

Satisfied With Variety, Amount?

Cucumber

This warm weather annual vine crop is grown throughout the United States. Cukes prefer fertile loam improved with well-rotted manure or compost to meet this crop's needs. A quarter-ounce of seed in a fifty-foot row will yield fifty pounds of cucumbers.

Planting: At least a week after the last frost, in a six-inch deep furrow, spread in a couple of inches of compost, or a bit of commercial fertilizer, cover with soil reaching within inch of top of furrow, spread seeds every eight inches, firm into soil with back of hoe, then cover with soil and firm again. Furrow must be in area where cucumber vines have six feet of running space.

Cultivation: Side-dress when vines reach stand-up stage. Keep soil moist at all times.

Harvesting: Cucumbers begin producing six to seven weeks after planting. Vines will produce until frost if cucumbers are picked before they reach yellow-ripe maturity, so keep them picked, even if they are not needed immediately. Early staminate or male blossoms appear first, and do not produce cucumbers. Small cucumbers can be seen below pistillate, or female blossoms. Pick slicing cucumbers when six to eight inches long, or even earlier, when there's something to eat.

Enemies: Cucumber beetles, both striped and twelve-spotted, will eat young plants, dine on leaves and stems of larger plants. Use malathion or Sevin, but not Sevin on young plants. Hotcaps or cheesecloth on frames over each plant will protect young plants. Fungus diseases such as downy mildew can be avoided by rotation of crops, control of insects, and selection of resistant seeds.

Varieties: The varieties include slicing and pickling cucumbers. Marketmore 70 (Sixty-five days, will produce crisp, flavorful eight-inch slicing cucumbers). Straight Eight (Fifty-eight days. Slicing. Does well in North). Spartan Valour (Sixty days. Slicing. Very slim, dark, and prolific). Wisconsin SMR 18 (Fifty-four days. Pickling. Good yield. Scab and mosaic disease resistant).

Suggestions: If you have an opportunity to grow cucumbers in a greenhouse, try one of the European varieties that are so expensive in supermarkets. They need lots of light, ample moisture, good soil. Given that, they'll produce rapidly and abundantly—on a good looking plant.

Straight and Clean

For the cleanest, straightest cucumbers in town, the ones easiest to pick and taking up the least space, grow cucumbers on a trellis. Make a trellis out of four-foot chicken wire with a wooden frame. One warning: The vines tend to dry out more quickly, so mulch heavily and water often.

Eggplant

This fussy plant is worth growing if only for the beauty of its fruit. It does well in a wide row. A delight for the gourmet, eggplant is very sensitive to cold weather, but this should not deter the gardener. Needs rich soil, with compost or rotted manure added. A good experimental crop for the gardener who has never tried it. Packet of seeds should produce fifty plants, double the number needed for even a family of eggplant lovers.

Planting: Start seeds indoors quarter-inch deep in flats or three-inch peat pots, seven to eight weeks in advance of transplanting time, which is week after last spring frost, and when soil is warm. Set plants out twelve inches apart in rows two to three feet apart. Plant in a 2-1-2 formation in a wide row. Shade plants for a day or two after planting.

Cultivation: Eggplants must be kept warm, moist, and fed from the moment of planting the seeds. The growth pattern should not be interrupted by lack of moisture or by cold. Keep weeds out of row, side-dress with compost, and mulch well, after plants have gotten a start in warm soil. Don't cultivate deeply. The roots are near the surface.

Harvesting: Admiration of the beauty of the fruit should not delay the harvest. Begin when fruits are small, cutting them from the stem. If fruits are left until they lose their gloss, the taste will suffer and the plant will stop producing.

Enemies: The Colorado potato beetle will desert potato vines to feast on your eggplants. Try rotenone. Sevin is effective. Spray, too, for aphids. Discourage cutworms with paper collars around stems. To avoid bacterial wilt, don't grow where potatoes, tomatoes, or eggplants have grown in the past three years.

Varieties: Black Beauty is the favorite (Seventy-three days from transplant to first mature fruit. Good producer of heavy, oval fruit). Ichiban (Sixty-five days) is a prolific producer of long and early fruit. To understand how eggplants got their name, grow a few of the ones with small, white fruit. Try Albino, Ornamental White, or White Beauty. They're fine to eat as well as being decorative.

Should You Peel?

It isn't necessary to peel eggplant, unless the eggplant you have is tough-skinned with age. Harvest when the eggplant is small, and leave the skin on.

19 ____

Planting   Variety   Date Planted   Amount Planted (Row Length)

1. _____   _____   _____

2. _____   _____   _____

3. _____   _____   _____

Harvest Dates   Variety   Expected   Actual

1. _____   _____   _____

2. _____   _____   _____

3. _____   _____   _____

Satisfied With Variety, Amount? _____

_____

19 ____

Planting   Variety   Date Planted   Amount Planted (Row Length)

1. _____   _____   _____

2. _____   _____   _____

3. _____   _____   _____

Harvest Dates   Variety   Expected   Actual

1. _____   _____   _____

2. _____   _____   _____

3. _____   _____   _____

Satisfied With Variety, Amount? _____

_____

19 ____

Planting   Variety   Date Planted   Amount Planted (Row Length)

1. _____   _____   _____

2. _____   _____   _____

3. _____   _____   _____

Harvest Dates   Variety   Expected   Actual

1. _____   _____   _____

2. _____   _____   _____

3. _____   _____   _____

Satisfied With Variety, Amount? _____

_____

19 ____

Planting	Variety	Date Planted	Amount Planted (Row Length)
1.			
2.			
3.			

Harvest Dates	Variety	Expected	Actual
1.			
2.			
3.			

Satisfied With Variety, Amount?

19 ____

Planting	Variety	Date Planted	Amount Planted (Row Length)
1.			
2.			
3.			

Harvest Dates	Variety	Expected	Actual
1.			
2.			
3.			

Satisfied With Variety, Amount?

19 ____

Planting	Variety	Date Planted	Amount Planted (Row Length)
1.			
2.			
3.			

Harvest Dates	Variety	Expected	Actual
1.			
2.			
3.			

Satisfied With Variety, Amount?

Garlic

This pungent member of the onion family grows one to two feet high. Does best in mild climates, in rich, sandy soil. A pound and a half of cloves will yield about twelve pounds of garlic.

Planting: Buy garlic bulbs in seed stores or the supermarket. When ready to plant, break cloves off bulb, and plant in a wide row, three to four inches apart, one inch deep, and the pointed end of the clove up. The larger, outer cloves will produce the larger bulbs. They can be planted in the early spring, but for a larger crop, plant in fall, and mulch heavily in the North for overwintering. In South or Southwest, plant cloves from fall through early spring.

Cultivation: Keep weed-free and mulched. Garlic plants are very shallow-rooted, so cultivate cautiously. If seed stalks form, break them off as soon as you notice them.

Harvesting: Harvest when tops turn brown and fall over. If garlic is in rich soil, and tops do not topple at the end of the season, bend them over. Pull up plants and let dry for a few days. Remove dried soil on them, and trim roots close to base.

Enemies: Same as onion. An onion maggot, the bad-breathed larva of a grey fly, eats into the bulb, and will cause it to rot. Burn any infested plants.

Suggestions: Garlic is a good vegetable to interplant, with a few cloves stuck in with cabbages, lettuce and other salad crops. I carry that one step further. My spaghetti sauce garden contains all of the spaghetti sauce ingredients that I can grow, and, of course, garlic is among them. Try to plant crops so that all these ingredients reach their peaks of perfection at just the right time for making the quantities of sauce that you will store for winter use.

Eau de Garlic

If the muscular scent of garlic lingers on your hands, scrub them with salt, then wash well with soap and water. And for the after-eating aroma, chew parsley.

Garlic Braids

A good way to store garlic is to braid it. Before the tops are entirely dry, try braiding them, adding cords to give strength to the braid. Hang the braids in a warm, shady place to cure, then store in a cool, dark place, bringing them out one at a time to decorate and provide garlic for the kitchen.

Kale

Kale, a member of the cabbage family, long was popular in the Northeast. Local growers could provide it to markets in the late fall, winter, and early spring, for a nutritious green. Then came the years of trucking lettuce thousands of miles, and kale took a back seat to this import from California and the states of the South. But now it's winning favor again. Nutritionists recognize its high vitamins A and C contents, and gardeners like its ability to grow tender and tasty after hard frosts, and even into the winter. An eighth of an ounce of seed will yield big harvests.

Planting: I plant kale in wide rows in July or August. It's a good crop to follow peas, which have enriched the soil. In the South, plant as late as October and enjoy fresh kale throughout the winter and on into the spring. When plants are up, thin them to 6-8 inches apart in the wide row.

Cultivation: As the plants grow, they'll need even more space. Harvest for eating. Make certain plants have plenty of nutrients and water, particularly water in hot weather, so that growth is fast and uninterrupted.

Harvesting: I harvest most of my kale in the fall, after the heavy frosts, and in early winter. We like it better than spinach, believe it's tastier and has more volume per plant. All of us, even the kids, like it, in soups, or cooked as greens, or with the tenderest leaves in salads. If we have deep snow or I mulch the plants heavily, kale will overwinter, for another harvest in early spring, when regrowth begins.

Enemies: Flea beetles usually are not a serious threat when weeds are eliminated. Cabbage worms can be troublesome. A late planting eliminates most problems. Or they can be eliminated with BT. See Broccoli.

Varieties: Vates (Sixty days to harvest. Attractive plant with finely curled bluish-green leaves). Blue Curled Scotch (Fifty-five days. Low compact plants. Winters well).

Suggestions: Try kale and enjoy a crop from the garden when almost everything else is gone and forgotten. Frost improves its flavor—it gets sweeter and more tender. For something different, dig up a Blue Curled Scotch plant, pot it, and display it as a houseplant, but use leaves for soups and garnishes.

Cooking with Kale

Tear the leaves from the stalks, wash, but don't soak, them, then drain well. For boiled kale, fry four strips of bacon with a half-cup of chopped onions. Bring a pot of salted water to a boil, add a large bunch of chopped kale, add the bacon, diced, and the onions, and cook until kale is just tender. Drain, and serve quickly with butter, seasonings, and a bit of vinegar or lemon juice.

19 ____

Planting	Variety	Date Planted	Amount Planted (Row Length)
1.	_____	_____	_____
2.	_____	_____	_____
3.	_____	_____	_____

Harvest Dates	Variety	Expected	Actual
1.	_____	_____	_____
2.	_____	_____	_____
3.	_____	_____	_____

Satisfied With Variety, Amount? _____

_____

19 ____

Planting	Variety	Date Planted	Amount Planted (Row Length)
1.	_____	_____	_____
2.	_____	_____	_____
3.	_____	_____	_____

Harvest Dates	Variety	Expected	Actual
1.	_____	_____	_____
2.	_____	_____	_____
3.	_____	_____	_____

Satisfied With Variety, Amount? _____

_____

19 ____

Planting	Variety	Date Planted	Amount Planted (Row Length)
1.	_____	_____	_____
2.	_____	_____	_____
3.	_____	_____	_____

Harvest Dates	Variety	Expected	Actual
1.	_____	_____	_____
2.	_____	_____	_____
3.	_____	_____	_____

Satisfied With Variety, Amount? _____

_____

19 ____

Planting	Variety	Date Planted	Amount Planted (Row Length)
1.			
2.			
3.			

Harvest Dates	Variety	Expected	Actual
1.			
2.			
3.			

Satisfied With Variety, Amount?

19 ____

Planting	Variety	Date Planted	Amount Planted (Row Length)
1.			
2.			
3.			

Harvest Dates	Variety	Expected	Actual
1.			
2.			
3.			

Satisfied With Variety, Amount?

19 ____

Planting	Variety	Date Planted	Amount Planted (Row Length)
1.			
2.			
3.			

Harvest Dates	Variety	Expected	Actual
1.			
2.			
3.			

Satisfied With Variety, Amount?

Kohlrabi

A novelty plant that's fun to eat. Peel and eat this aboveground turnip like an apple, peel and slice it and offer it with dips, add slices to salads, stir-fry it, or cook it with a cream sauce. It's easy to grow, and good in a variety of dishes. A half-ounce of seed will yield thirty pounds.

Planting: Can be started indoors, six weeks before planting date, which is one week before the expected last spring frost. Or plant outside, with seeds a half-inch deep and four inches apart. You can plant in a wide row, too, and thin plants to three to five inches apart.

Cultivation: Kohlrabi is an amiable vegetable. It does well on almost any soil, and at almost any temperature. Keep it free of weeds and well watered and you'll have a fine crop.

Harvesting: Kohlrabi will produce its swollen stem, the part to eat, in seven to eight weeks. Pick them when they're 1½ to 2 inches thick; they begin to get woody and have a bitter taste soon after that. Kohlrabi can be harvested for weeks after the first frost.

Enemies: Has the same enemies as cabbage, but most are discouraged by good cultivation.

Varieties: Early White Vienna (Fifty-five days to harvesting. Mild flavor. Creamy white flesh). Early Purple Vienna (Sixty days. Purple bulbs, greenish white flesh. These bulbs may be grown slightly larger than Early Whites before eating).

Suggestions: If you need new ways to serve kohlrabi, try any recipes that call for turnips, and substitute. You'll find the dish has a slight flavor of cabbage it lacked when made with turnip. Try the young foliage of kohlrabi, too. Cook it as a rather pungent green.

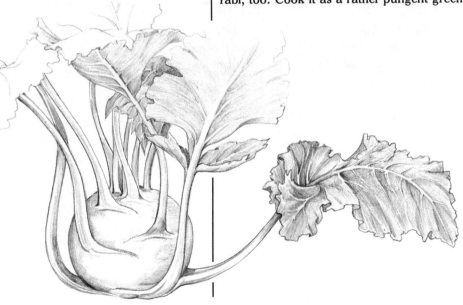

Leeks

Leeks require a long season to reach the size of those found in markets. Don't despair if yours are smaller. They're just as tasty, and often are more tender. Leeks look like oversize green onions. They must be blanched to achieve that white lower stem so favored by the best of cooks.

Planting: To give leeks a good start in the North, sow seeds in flats, one inch apart, and half an inch deep, three months before the last frost. I start mine in February, and, as I do with onions, I keep the tops cut back. I set them out four to six inches apart and one inch deeper than they grew, in the bottom of a six-inch deep furrow, about the time of the last frost. You can make two of these furrows running lengthwise on a raised bed or wide row. In the South, you can sow seeds or set out transplants in the fall.

Cultivation: Gradually fill in furrow, as the leeks grow, to blanch them and thus make them more tender. As they reach full growth, bank entire stem with sand or compost. If plants are in a wide row or raised bed, it's possible to add several inches of compost, soil, or leaves to blanket the bed.

Harvesting: If you have a lot of leeks, harvest some of them early in the summer as scallions, or use them as leeks, adding five small ones for every big one called for in a recipe. For late fall use, leeks may be left in the ground until after a heavy frost, then dug, packed closely, and stored in an unheated building. Late-started crops can be overwintered by mulching heavily with hay or straw, and they will produce a delicious spring crop.

Enemies: Leeks have few enemies, and are easily grown. If rot is detected, onion maggot, the larva of a small, grey fly, may be responsible. Destroy those plants.

Varieties: American Flag (120 days to maturity. Fine for fall and winter). Broad London (130 days. Good in South).

Suggestions: Banking the leeks with soil or compost tends to force sand into the layers of each plant. Wash carefully under running water, and split each leek lengthwise to wash out if sand is particularly troublesome.

19 _____

Planting   Variety   Date Planted   Amount Planted (Row Length)

1. _____   _____   _____

2. _____   _____   _____

3. _____   _____   _____

Harvest Dates   Variety   Expected   Actual

1. _____   _____   _____

2. _____   _____   _____

3. _____   _____   _____

Satisfied With Variety, Amount? _____

_____

19 _____

Planting   Variety   Date Planted   Amount Planted (Row Length)

1. _____   _____   _____

2. _____   _____   _____

3. _____   _____   _____

Harvest Dates   Variety   Expected   Actual

1. _____   _____   _____

2. _____   _____   _____

3. _____   _____   _____

Satisfied With Variety, Amount? _____

_____

19 _____

Planting   Variety   Date Planted   Amount Planted (Row Length)

1. _____   _____   _____

2. _____   _____   _____

3. _____   _____   _____

Harvest Dates   Variety   Expected   Actual

1. _____   _____   _____

2. _____   _____   _____

3. _____   _____   _____

Satisfied With Variety, Amount? _____

_____

19 ____

Planting	Variety	Date Planted	Amount Planted (Row Length)
1.	_____	_____	_____
2.	_____	_____	_____
3.	_____	_____	_____

Harvest Dates	Variety	Expected	Actual
1.	_____	_____	_____
2.	_____	_____	_____
3.	_____	_____	_____

Satisfied With Variety, Amount? _____

_____

19 ____

Planting	Variety	Date Planted	Amount Planted (Row Length)
1.	_____	_____	_____
2.	_____	_____	_____
3.	_____	_____	_____

Harvest Dates	Variety	Expected	Actual
1.	_____	_____	_____
2.	_____	_____	_____
3.	_____	_____	_____

Satisfied With Variety, Amount? _____

_____

19 ____

Planting	Variety	Date Planted	Amount Planted (Row Length)
1.	_____	_____	_____
2.	_____	_____	_____
3.	_____	_____	_____

Harvest Dates	Variety	Expected	Actual
1.	_____	_____	_____
2.	_____	_____	_____
3.	_____	_____	_____

Satisfied With Variety, Amount? _____

_____

Lettuce, Loose-Leaf

Raise just a little lettuce—but a lot of times. Plant different varieties, and start lettuce at two-week intervals, so there is top-quality lettuce for the table at all times. Lettuce does best in cool temperatures—spring and fall—in rich, well-watered soil.

Planting: To eat homegrown lettuce as early in the season as possible, start indoors six weeks before last spring frost. When ground can be worked, transplant outside, and at same time plant seeds outdoors. Lettuce is an ideal crop for raised beds and wide rows. Set out transplants in a 3-2-3 formation, eight inches apart. Cover seeds with a quarter-inch of soil. Raise only short sections of a wide row or raised bed, such as three to five feet for each variety, or about twenty feet for any variety in a single row. In late summer start the fall crop.

Cultivating: Thin the seeded section of the wide row to give remaining plants room to grow. Keep soil moist, ground free of weeds, so growth isn't interrupted.

Harvesting: Begin harvest as soon as leaves are big enough to eat. To get maximum amount of lettuce, cut off plant an inch above ground. That way, you'll get at least two harvests from the same plant, as plants send up new growth. If it's cool and damp, you may get five harvests. Lettuce is crispest in the morning, the best time to harvest.

Enemies: Rot at base of plants is usually due to overcrowding. Rotation urged to avoid fungus and bacterial diseases. Slugs dislike scatterings of wood ashes or lime, and will give up their lives for a short beer in a saucer.

Varieties: Try a lot of them. Salad Bowl (Forty-five days to maturity. Crisp and tender. Almost foolproof for a good crop). Black Seeded Simpson (Forty-five days. Great taste). Ruby (Fifty days. Adds color to your garden and your salad bowl). Oak Leaf (Forty days. One of the more heat-resistant of leaf lettuces).

Suggestions: In hot weather, grow plants in the shade—on the north side of the cucumber trellis, behind those towering bean poles, or under bean tepees or broccoli plants. Or stretch cheesecloth across a section of a wide row.

Try sprinkling black pepper to discourage hungry rabbits.

Lettuce, Head

There are two varieties, the crisphead types so common in the supermarket, and butterheads, with looser, greener heads and more taste and vitamins. You can grow both in your garden, although crispheads may be less perfect than the commercial varieties. Crispheads are more difficult to grow, but you can get a good crop if you start early and harvest before hot weather.

Planting: Start both inside, six weeks before a last frost, which is the ideal time to set out transplants. Set them in a 3-2-3 formation in a wide row, eight to ten inches apart. In mid-summer, start a fall crop of butterhead lettuce. In the South, gardeners aiming for a fall crop sow seed in a bed in early August, and transplant as soon as plants are large enough. The bed is partially shaded and kept well watered. The crop will head from late October to late December. For a spring crop in the South, lettuce is often sown in cold frames from early November to late January, depending on the location and weather. Plants are set out from January to March and harvested beginning in about two months.

Cultivation: Mulch with compost to keep weeds down. Keep well watered. Wide rows keep soil cool, and cool soil is what lettuce loves.

Harvesting: Harvest some heads before they reach full growth, to give others in a wide row room to expand.

Enemies: See Lettuce, Loose-leafed.

Varieties: This is only a sample of the many excellent varieties available, Ithaca (ninety days). Great Lakes (Ninety days to mature head. Heavy crisphead type and good quality. Stands up well to heat). Buttercrunch (Seventy-five days. Favorite of many. A superior butterhead, tasty, crisp, and slow to bolt). Dark Green Boston (Eighty days. Delicious butterhead).

Suggestions: I find that I can grow better head lettuce if I start all varieties as transplants. The plants look better, and it's possible to space them more carefully, for better development. All of these varieties will do well in the shade of pole bean tepees and under broccoli.

10"   10"

10"

Try planting head lettuce in this formation.

19 ____

Planting	Variety	Date Planted	Amount Planted (Row Length)
1.			
2.			
3.			

Harvest Dates	Variety	Expected	Actual
1.			
2.			
3.			

Satisfied With Variety, Amount?

19 ____

Planting	Variety	Date Planted	Amount Planted (Row Length)
1.			
2.			
3.			

Harvest Dates	Variety	Expected	Actual
1.			
2.			
3.			

Satisfied With Variety, Amount?

19 ____

Planting	Variety	Date Planted	Amount Planted (Row Length)
1.			
2.			
3.			

Harvest Dates	Variety	Expected	Actual
1.			
2.			
3.			

Satisfied With Variety, Amount?

19 ____

Planting   Variety   Date Planted   Amount Planted (Row Length)

1. _____   _____   _____

2. _____   _____   _____

3. _____   _____   _____

Harvest Dates   Variety   Expected   Actual

1. _____   _____   _____

2. _____   _____   _____

3. _____   _____   _____

Satisfied With Variety, Amount?

_____

_____

---

19 ____

Planting   Variety   Date Planted   Amount Planted (Row Length)

1. _____   _____   _____

2. _____   _____   _____

3. _____   _____   _____

Harvest Dates   Variety   Expected   Actual

1. _____   _____   _____

2. _____   _____   _____

3. _____   _____   _____

Satisfied With Variety, Amount?

_____

_____

---

19 ____

Planting   Variety   Date Planted   Amount Planted (Row Length)

1. _____   _____   _____

2. _____   _____   _____

3. _____   _____   _____

Harvest Dates   Variety   Expected   Actual

1. _____   _____   _____

2. _____   _____   _____

3. _____   _____   _____

Satisfied With Variety, Amount?

_____

_____

Muskmelon

The perfect melon, juicy and tasty, is the Holy Grail of many gardeners, and it's elusive, too. That perfect melon demands the right variety for the area, a good start in the spring, rich, moist, sandy soil, room enough to stretch out vines, freedom from disease and insects, and a long season of sunny, warm weather and tropical nights. If you have clay soil, try preparing raised beds, adding lots of compost and organic matter to the soil. A fifty-foot row should yield thirty melons.

Planting: Start seeds inside in peat pots three weeks before planting time. This lengthens the short seasons of the North, makes melons ripen before the hot, dry periods in the South. Plant outside a week after last frost date, when soil is warm. Carefully remove the peat pot, not disturbing the roots, before planting. Plant in row ten to twelve inches apart. Space rows six feet apart. Protect, if necessary, with hotcaps or plastic grow tunnels.

Cultivation: Melons are shallow-rooted, so cultivate carefully and mulch when soil is warm. Avoid moving vines. Remove melons that set late in the season, to improve the size and quality of the earlier ones. To hasten growing and ripening, set small melons on coffee cans.

Harvesting: Musk melons are ready to be eaten when they are at "slip" stage, and slight pressure on vine will cause melon to slip off. Some gardeners kneel down and sniff end for a rich, fruity smell that tells them the melon is ready.

Enemies: Starting melons indoors lessens chance of trouble from striped cucumber beetle, which attacks seedlings and spreads fusarium wilt. Hotcaps, fine for warming area around plant, will also help to protect from these beetles. Downy and powdery mildew are worse in wet weather. Varieties tolerant to both mildew and wilt are available.

Varieties: Remember to find which melons do best in your area. In Southwest, for example, honeydews love that hot, dry climate, but don't produce as well in the South. My favorites are Ambrosia (Eighty-six days. Very sweet, with thick meat) and Alaska (Seventy days. An early producer that's tops in flavor).

Suggestions: I planted an experimental crop of melons, with half of them on black plastic. The soil for them was warmer, of course. Results: I had twice as many fruit three to four weeks earlier, from those on plastic. In this country, almost any muskmelon is called a cantaloupe, but the truth is they're not the same. True cantaloupes have hard, warted rind and are seldom grown in the United States. With their netted, yellow or green skin, muskmelons have assumed the identity of their European cousin.

Okra

This relative of the showy hibiscus flower grows three to six or more feet high. It produces beautiful blooms, then the immature pods which are fried, cooked in soups, stews, and meat dishes, or pickled. Also called gumbo. A standby in southern cooking, okra also will grow well in the North—and is well worth growing, too, if only for those lovely blossoms. An ounce of seed will provide thirty pounds of okra every two weeks—and that's a lot of okra.

Planting: A week or two after the last spring frost, when the soil is good and warm, sow seeds half-inch deep, eight inches apart, three or four seeds to a hill, with hills eighteen inches apart, in rows three feet apart. When seedlings are two inches tall, thin to leave sixteen to twenty-four inches between plants. Can also be started in peat pots, a month in advance, putting two seeds in each pot, and later cutting off the weaker seedling. When night temperatures remain above 50°, plant pots sixteen inches apart, in rows three feet apart.

Cultivation: Keep free of weeds. Mulch with compost.

Harvesting: When pods are three to four inches long, they should be picked. They become tough and useless when five to six inches long. If pods are allowed to become mature (seven to nine inches), plants will stop producing.

Enemies: Hand pick the green stinkbugs and cabbage loopers that often are found in okra.

Varieties: Clemson Spineless (Fifty-five days from planting to first edible pods. Good producer. Four-foot plants. The overwhelming favorite). Red Okra (Sixty days). Plants grow five to six feet tall). Perkins Spineless (Fifty-three days. The brown-green pods are thinner than Clemson. Plants grow 4½-6 feet tall).

Suggestions: I've had the best success with okra in my northern garden raising it in a double-size plastic tunnel where soil temperatures will soar above 90° even on a coolish day. They soon outgrow the tunnel, but this gets them off to a good start. And for a refreshing change in colors, try raising Red Okra.

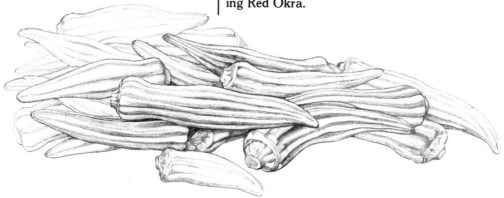

19 ____

Planting	Variety	Date Planted	Amount Planted (Row Length)
1.			
2.			
3.			

Harvest Dates	Variety	Expected	Actual
1.			
2.			
3.			

Satisfied With Variety, Amount?

---

19 ____

Planting	Variety	Date Planted	Amount Planted (Row Length)
1.			
2.			
3.			

Harvest Dates	Variety	Expected	Actual
1.			
2.			
3.			

Satisfied With Variety, Amount?

---

19 ____

Planting	Variety	Date Planted	Amount Planted (Row Length)
1.			
2.			
3.			

Harvest Dates	Variety	Expected	Actual
1.			
2.			
3.			

Satisfied With Variety, Amount?

19 _____

Planting	Variety	Date Planted	Amount Planted (Row Length)
1.			
2.			
3.			

Harvest Dates	Variety	Expected	Actual
1.			
2.			
3.			

Satisfied With Variety, Amount?

_____

_____

19 _____

Planting	Variety	Date Planted	Amount Planted (Row Length)
1.			
2.			
3.			

Harvest Dates	Variety	Expected	Actual
1.			
2.			
3.			

Satisfied With Variety, Amount?

_____

_____

19 _____

Planting	Variety	Date Planted	Amount Planted (Row Length)
1.			
2.			
3.			

Harvest Dates	Variety	Expected	Actual
1.			
2.			
3.			

Satisfied With Variety, Amount?

_____

_____

Onions

Onions are essential in my garden. Gardeners should try several varieties. They grow anywhere in the United States, produce well in limited space. Rare is the gardener who raises too many. In planning on storage, it should be remembered that the stronger the flavor, the longer the onion will keep. Fertile, moist soil is needed. The gardener has a choice of raising from seeds, plants, or sets (tiny onions started the previous season).

Planting: Seeds should be started indoors ten to twelve weeks in advance of transplanting. Start seeds in a flat with four to five inches of soil or starter mix. Try to keep seeds a quarter-inch apart, or thin to that distance. Cover with a light layer of soil, then wrap flat in plastic and cover with newspaper. Keep in temperature range of 65°-70°. When seeds sprout, remove newspapers and plastic. Whenever plants reach three inches high, cut them back to one inch, so plants develop strong roots. Plant outside after final frost. Plant sets or plants at this time also. For an impressive sight, plant a wide row or raised bed that's three to four feet wide.

Cultivation: Keep free of weeds, particularly when first started. Side-dress when six to eight inches high, again when bulbs begin to form.

Harvesting: Pull up when tops turn brown. Leave in garden during sunny days, for two or three days, until they are dry. Then break off roots. To cure, spread them out in a warm, airy, shaded place until the roots are dry and brittle and skin becomes papery. Eat thick-stemmed ones first. They won't keep as long. Put others in a mesh bag, and hang in a cool, dry area. When cutting off tops, leave about an inch at the neck.

Enemies: It is not often that the home gardener is troubled with either pests or disease in the onion rows. Onion maggot, a tiny, white worm-like creature, may attack seedlings, making them rot. If they invade larger onions, which are stored, they will cause a rot that will spread to others stored. Destroy onions where this is detected. Stop thrips with Sevin.

Varieties: In the North, Early Yellow Globe (100 days. Good for either a summer or fall crop). Southport Yellow Globe (115 days). In South, Granex (105 days. Early yellow bulb that's a good keeper). Texas Early Grano 502 (Resistant to thrips). If you plant sets, try Stuttgarter (120 days) and Yellow Ebenezer (100 days).

Suggestions: Onions are a good companion crop. Plant a few in with other vegetables, such as lettuce, and pick them in all stages, from scallions, before they develop bulbs, to the mature onion. If you like scallions, plant onion sets only an inch and a half apart in wide rows. Harvest every other one as a scallion. The rest will develop into large onions.

Parsnips

Most often grown in the North, since a heavy frost or freezing is needed to improve the flavor of the roots. Very slow to germinate and equally leisurely in growth. Need a light soil, worked deeply, and rich in organic matter. Use fresh seeds each year. A half-ounce of seed will yield fifty pounds of parsnips. An ideal crop for the wide row or raised bed.

Planting: About the date of the last spring frost, sow seeds rather thickly, toss in a few radish seeds to mark the location, and cover with a half-inch of soil. The radish seeds will push growth up through any crust that forms on the soil, a crust that could halt the growth of the parsnips. The parsnip seeds may take as long as twenty days to germinate. Parsnips do best in a raised bed, where the soft soil invites the roots to grow large.

Cultivation: In a wide row or a narrow row, keep the growing parsnips three to four inches apart. Keep plant bed moist, particularly while waiting for tiny plants to appear.

Harvesting: May be harvested in the fall, or mulched heavily and harvested during the winter, or—and this is the usual way—dug up in the spring. The cold turns the carbohydrates to sugar. Dig deeply and carefully when harvesting this large, brittle root. Unlike many other root crops, the large roots are just as meaty and tasty as the smaller ones.

Enemies: Parsnips are sometimes bothered by carrot rust fly, the maggot of which eats into roots of parsnips, celery, and carrots. If this is a problem in your area, delay planting for a few weeks, or cover young plants with cheesecloth draped on a frame.

Varieties: Hollow Crown (105 days. Broad, tapered twelve-inch roots. Heavy yield). Harris Model (120 days. Roots are ten to twelve inches long. Smooth, white flesh).

Suggestions: In medieval days, parsnips and apples were chopped up and made into fritters. The same combination, in dishes ranging from stuffings to dessert, is still popular. To grow parsnips requires patience, but they're well worth waiting for.

The Perfect Parsnips

A friend of mine in southern Vermont had trouble growing parsnips. They were short and crooked, made so by the rocky, hard soil of his garden. To grow better parsnips, he experimented. He used a short steel bar, plunging it a foot into the ground, then whirling it around, to form a cone. He did this the length of a row, filled the cone-shaped holes with his best compost, and planted his parsnips in them. That fall he had parsnips that Burpee would envy.

19 ____

Planting   Variety   Date Planted   Amount Planted (Row Length)

1. _____   _____   _____

2. _____   _____   _____

3. _____   _____   _____

Harvest Dates   Variety   Expected   Actual

1. _____   _____   _____

2. _____   _____   _____

3. _____   _____   _____

Satisfied With Variety, Amount? _____

_____

19 ____

Planting   Variety   Date Planted   Amount Planted (Row Length)

1. _____   _____   _____

2. _____   _____   _____

3. _____   _____   _____

Harvest Dates   Variety   Expected   Actual

1. _____   _____   _____

2. _____   _____   _____

3. _____   _____   _____

Satisfied With Variety, Amount? _____

_____

19 ____

Planting   Variety   Date Planted   Amount Planted (Row Length)

1. _____   _____   _____

2. _____   _____   _____

3. _____   _____   _____

Harvest Dates   Variety   Expected   Actual

1. _____   _____   _____

2. _____   _____   _____

3. _____   _____   _____

Satisfied With Variety, Amount? _____

_____

19 ____

Planting	Variety	Date Planted	Amount Planted (Row Length)
1.	_____	_____	_____
2.	_____	_____	_____
3.	_____	_____	_____

Harvest Dates	Variety	Expected	Actual
1.	_____	_____	_____
2.	_____	_____	_____
3.	_____	_____	_____

Satisfied With Variety, Amount? _____
_____

19 ____

Planting	Variety	Date Planted	Amount Planted (Row Length)
1.	_____	_____	_____
2.	_____	_____	_____
3.	_____	_____	_____

Harvest Dates	Variety	Expected	Actual
1.	_____	_____	_____
2.	_____	_____	_____
3.	_____	_____	_____

Satisfied With Variety, Amount? _____
_____

19 ____

Planting	Variety	Date Planted	Amount Planted (Row Length)
1.	_____	_____	_____
2.	_____	_____	_____
3.	_____	_____	_____

Harvest Dates	Variety	Expected	Actual
1.	_____	_____	_____
2.	_____	_____	_____
3.	_____	_____	_____

Satisfied With Variety, Amount? _____
_____

Peanuts

Easy to grow in the South, with few enemies. A challenge for northern gardeners, but a challenge more and more are accepting, and they're succeeding in their efforts. Acid, light sandy soil with high organic material content is needed. Most peanuts require four to five months to grow.

Planting: The big question for novice growers is how far to undress the peanut before planting it. The answer is that you can plant the peanut, husk and all. But for faster germination, remove the husk, but not the thin skin of the individual nut. And be careful not to crack the peanut. In North or South, try a raised bed for peanuts. The warmer soil stimulates growth, the soft soil makes it easy for the plant to complete its growth cycle. In South, plant after the last frost; in the North, about the time of the last frost. Plant peanuts one to two inches deep, and place them three to six inches apart. In a wide row, make two rows, eighteen inches apart.

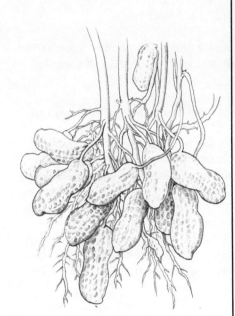

Cultivation: Plants grow 1-1½ feet high, produce flowers on stems that bend, touch ground, then root themselves into the ground. Peanuts then form in clusters underground. When plants are a foot high, hill them, pulling soil up around them, then mulch between the rows. Make sure plants have ample water when they're in bloom.

Harvesting: In South, dig vines with a garden fork before frost, cure the peanuts about two months in an open shed. In the North, in mid-October dig the vines and hang them in attic or some other dry place. Plant signals when peanuts are ready for harvest by turning yellow. Cure peanuts about two months, then they can be stored. Roast nuts twenty minutes in a 300° F. oven.

Enemies: Leaf spot is common when weather is hot and damp. Potato leaf hoppers, which feed on leaves, will spread disease. Use pyrethrum or malathion.

Varieties: Early Spanish (100 days. Perfect for short-season areas. Small nuts). Spanish (110 days. Dwarf bushes. Heavy bearers of small nuts with a grand flavor). Jumbo Virginia (120 days. Larger vines, some spreading 3½ feet. Large, tasty peanuts).

Suggestions: Try peanuts if you have a children's garden. They love to watch them grow, love roasting them, love eating them.

Peas

In Thomas Jefferson's day, he and his neighbors vied to see who could grow the earliest peas. The winner was host at a dinner at which the peas, Jefferson's favorite vegetable, were featured. Peas have retained their popularity, and now are much easier to grow. Can be grown in most of the United States, but do best in cool climates. One of the best crops for wide rows and raised beds. Rich, sandy loam is best. Half-pound of peas should yield at least thirty pounds. Tall varieties require support such as fence or branches four to five feet long.

Planting: Dust seed with nitrogen inoculant. As soon as ground can be worked, plant seeds one inch deep, spaced two to three inches apart, with rows three feet apart. In wide rows, scatter seeds three to four inches apart, and rake a one-inch layer of soil over them. Soaking peas before planting is recommended only if ground is dry. Instead of successive plantings for longer harvest, plant early and later varieties at the same time. For wide row, plant short-stemmed varieties, such as Little Marvel and Progress #9, that require no support.

Cultivation: Keep weeds out of young plants. Irrigate if spring rain doesn't provide enough moisture, and make certain there is enough moisture in critical period when pods are filling out. Mulch rows.

Harvesting: Harvest when pods are young and tender, and as soon as they are well filled, but before they begin to turn color. Shell and cook as soon after picking as possible.

Enemies: Malathion will halt any aphids that cause trouble, which is rare.

Varieties: Experiment each year until you find the ideal pea for your soil conditions, temperatures, and taste, recording your successes and failures. Little Marvel (Sixty-three days from planting to eating. Eighteen-inch high bushes. Tasty both fresh and frozen). Progress #9 (Sixty days. Resistant to fusarium wilt. Productive and delicious). Lincoln (Seventy-five days. This is for the gourmet who will wait a few days for the best. Heavy crop).

Suggestions: For a hedge of peas, try the Novella in a row that's as wide as your rake. This leafless variety forms a neat hedge that looks as if it has been clipped. Peas are delicious.

No-Care Peas

For no-care pea growing, try this:

Very early in the season, till up a ten-foot square of your garden. Scatter on it one pound of a shorter-bushed pea, such as Little Marvel. Till or rake them in. And that's it until two months later when you return to harvest them—and you should harvest fifty pounds of pods from that tiny space. No need for fences or other supports—the peas will support each other.

19 ____

Planting   Variety   Date Planted   Amount Planted (Row Length)

1. _____   _____   _____

2. _____   _____   _____

3. _____   _____   _____

Harvest Dates   Variety   Expected   Actual

1. _____   _____   _____

2. _____   _____   _____

3. _____   _____   _____

Satisfied With Variety, Amount? _____

_____

---

19 ____

Planting   Variety   Date Planted   Amount Planted (Row Length)

1. _____   _____   _____

2. _____   _____   _____

3. _____   _____   _____

Harvest Dates   Variety   Expected   Actual

1. _____   _____   _____

2. _____   _____   _____

3. _____   _____   _____

Satisfied With Variety, Amount? _____

_____

---

19 ____

Planting   Variety   Date Planted   Amount Planted (Row Length)

1. _____   _____   _____

2. _____   _____   _____

3. _____   _____   _____

Harvest Dates   Variety   Expected   Actual

1. _____   _____   _____

2. _____   _____   _____

3. _____   _____   _____

Satisfied With Variety, Amount? _____

_____

19 _____

Planting   Variety   Date Planted   Amount Planted (Row Length)

1. _____   _____   _____
2. _____   _____   _____
3. _____   _____   _____

Harvest Dates   Variety   Expected   Actual

1. _____   _____   _____
2. _____   _____   _____
3. _____   _____   _____

Satisfied With Variety, Amount? _____

_____

19 _____

Planting   Variety   Date Planted   Amount Planted (Row Length)

1. _____   _____   _____
2. _____   _____   _____
3. _____   _____   _____

Harvest Dates   Variety   Expected   Actual

1. _____   _____   _____
2. _____   _____   _____
3. _____   _____   _____

Satisfied With Variety, Amount? _____

_____

19 _____

Planting   Variety   Date Planted   Amount Planted (Row Length)

1. _____   _____   _____
2. _____   _____   _____
3. _____   _____   _____

Harvest Dates   Variety   Expected   Actual

1. _____   _____   _____
2. _____   _____   _____
3. _____   _____   _____

Satisfied With Variety, Amount? _____

_____

Peppers

Grow lots of these, and try many varieties. There are the hot ones that seem to grow hotter as they change color, and the blocky fruit varieties, called sweet, bell, or green peppers. The sweet pepper is usually eaten green, but its vitamin C content increases if it's left on the plant to turn red. Peppers prefer a mellow loam, but do well in any fertile, well-drained soil. One plant will often yield a pound or more of peppers. For a feature of your garden that will attract admiration, try a wide row of pepper plants, aligned in a 3-2-3 formation, twelve to fourteen inches apart, or in a narrower wide row in a 2-1-2 formation.

Planting: Start plants indoors six to eight weeks in advance of transplanting time, which is at least one week after the last spring frost. Start in flats or in three-inch peat pots, with seeds half-inch deep. Set out plants twelve to fourteen inches apart, in rows thirty inches apart, or in wide rows or on raised beds. Water well and, if sunny and hot, shade after transplanting. Relatively quick-growing crops, such as radishes or green onions, can be planted with the peppers, and harvested before pepper plants reach their full growth.

Cultivation: Peppers develop at their own pace, and the gardener should not be worried if at times the plants seem to do nothing for days. After the ground is warm, mulch to keep down weeds and save moisture. Some recommend black plastic mulch, because it tends to make soil warmer, and warm soil is what peppers like. Plants may need watering in the first few weeks after setting out, but usually not after that.

Harvesting: Both sweet and hot peppers are good to eat at all stages of growth. Cut peppers off plant with knife or scissors, half-inch from pepper cap. Sweet varieties are excellent for freezing.

Enemies: Use newspaper collars around tiny plants to thwart the cutworms. Most other troubles will be prevented if gardener keeps weeds out of plants and doesn't walk around them when the plants are wet. If you have husky, dark green pepper plants and no peppers, you've overfed them with a nitrogen-rich fertilizer. If they have blossoms, but don't bear peppers, blame that cold spell, and wait for further blossoms. All peppers should be side-dressed when they blossom. See side-dressing table on page 30. Limit amount of commerical fertilizer to a teaspoon per plant.

Varieties: Gedeon (Seventy-eight days. Huge, elongated fruit. A sweet variety that's great for stuffing or freezing). California Wonder (Seventy-five days. Sweet). Sweet Banana (Seventy-two days. Yellow to orange to red). Sweet Cherry (Seventy-eight days. Great for pickling whole). Long Red Cayenne (Seventy-two days. Hot. Easily dried). Hungarian Wax (Sixty-five days. Hot Yellow, changing to red. Six-inch fruit).

Suggestions: Peppers, with their shiny leaves and fruits of several colors, are one of the most attractive of vegetables. Plant a few with flowers in your border. Perfect for pots and other containers.

For more peppers, spray blossoms with 1 teaspoon of Epsom salts in 1 pint of water.

Potatoes

Garden books often suggest home gardeners should not raise potatoes since they take up a lot of room and, unlike corn, peas, or tomatoes, aren't much better than store-bought varieties. But this means you'll miss the taste of small, new potatoes, and the surprises in the fall of digging into each hill to see how many there will be. Try planting ten pounds and judge for yourself. Need mellow, fertile, acid, well-drained soil, not limed nor fertilized with fresh manure. Five pounds of potatoes in a fifty-foot row should produce more than fifty pounds.

Planting: Two days before planting, cut seed potatoes (for best results make sure they're certified seed potatoes) into blocky chunks, each with at least two eyes. Dig eight-inch deep trenches, thirty-six inches apart. Add a two-inch layer of compost, plus some superphosphate, about a handful per foot, to the bottom of the trench. Cover with two inches of soil. Place potato chunks cut side down and ten to twelve inches apart. Cover with four inches of soil.

Cultivation: Start hilling as soon as plants emerge. Pull soil into trench around growing plants, then cover them right up. Hilling kills the weeds, allows developing tubers to expand, and keeps emerging potatoes from turning green from the sun. Do this at least twice.

Harvesting: Two weeks after blossoms form, start harvesting some of those small, early potatoes—they're delicious. For storage, allow potatoes to mature, and harvest when most of tops have died back. Dig when soil is dry. Dry potatoes for a few hours outside, then store in a dark room with high humidity and temperatures of thirty-six to forty.

Enemies: Potatoes can have as many as sixty diseases. But no crop yet has had all of them, and most can be avoided by following a few rules. Don't grow potatoes where tomatoes, eggplant, or peppers (or potatoes, of course) have grown in the past three years. Don't add lime or fresh manure to soil. Plant certified disease-free potatoes. To combat Colorado potato beetles, pick them off, use rotenone, or Sevin according to instructions.

Varieties: Plant area favorites. Norland (Eighty days. Early. Red-skinned. Resistant to scab). Kennebec (110 days. Late maturing. An old reliable). Katahdin (110 days. Late maturing. Good keeper).

Suggestions: Plants can take some insect damage. But don't let all foliage be eaten before taking action. And look on the underside of leaves for bright orange dots—the eggs of the Colorado potato beetle. Green potatoes contain solanine, which can be toxic. Remove green part before eating. Storing potatoes in the dark will prevent greening.

Cut seed potatoes into chunks each with two or three buds.

19 ____

Planting	Variety	Date Planted	Amount Planted (Row Length)
1.			
2.			
3.			

Harvest Dates	Variety	Expected	Actual
1.			
2.			
3.			

Satisfied With Variety, Amount?

19 ____

Planting	Variety	Date Planted	Amount Planted (Row Length)
1.			
2.			
3.			

Harvest Dates	Variety	Expected	Actual
1.			
2.			
3.			

Satisfied With Variety, Amount?

19 ____

Planting	Variety	Date Planted	Amount Planted (Row Length)
1.			
2.			
3.			

Harvest Dates	Variety	Expected	Actual
1.			
2.			
3.			

Satisfied With Variety, Amount?

19 ____

Planting	Variety	Date Planted	Amount Planted (Row Length)
1.			
2.			
3.			

Harvest Dates	Variety	Expected	Actual
1.			
2.			
3.			

Satisfied With Variety, Amount?

_____

_____

19 ____

Planting	Variety	Date Planted	Amount Planted (Row Length)
1.			
2.			
3.			

Harvest Dates	Variety	Expected	Actual
1.			
2.			
3.			

Satisfied With Variety, Amount?

_____

_____

19 ____

Planting	Variety	Date Planted	Amount Planted (Row Length)
1.			
2.			
3.			

Harvest Dates	Variety	Expected	Actual
1.			
2.			
3.			

Satisfied With Variety, Amount?

_____

_____

Pumpkin

When I'm planning my garden, pumpkins are the only vegetable my children ask me to plant. This sprawling squash plant is as intruding as a borrowing neighbor, but it must be raised if there are young members in the family. Scratch their names on their "own" young pumpkins and those names will appear large and plain at Halloween. As a space-saving maneuver, interplant with sweet corn, if you don't mind tripping over vines as you gather the corn. Grown throughout the United States. Stronger in flavor than squash, so less popular, but can be used in pies and bread. Likes rich, light soil.

Planting: Prepare rows eight to ten feet apart. Dig in plenty of compost or well-rotted manure. Two weeks after last frost, plant seeds one inch deep eight to ten inches apart.

Cultivation: Mulch heavily and keep well watered. Once vines have set several fruit, pinch back vines to direct growth into fruit more than foliage.

Harvesting: Pumpkins may disappear if not harvested before Halloween. After light frost, but before hard frost, cut them from vine with sharp knife, leaving a three-inch handle. Allow to cure for two or three weeks in a warm, well-ventilated place. Store in a cool, dry cellar.

Enemies: This is a hardy plant, well able to take care of itself if given a good start. Squash vine borer can be troublesome. If branch of vine wilts, cut into where wilt begins, and dig him out. In heat of day, check for squash bugs, and crush any found.

Varieties: Connecticut Field (110 days. Coarse and sweet meat. A good general-purpose pumpkin; weighs fifteen to twenty-five pounds). Small Sugar (100 days. Best flavored. Weighs about seven pounds. A good one to grow). Cinderella (Ninety-five days. Ten-inch pumpkins. Grows on a bush-like plant that can be restrained into a six-square-foot area).

Suggestions: To save space, train the vines to a fence. The vine and tendrils will grow extra strong to support the weight of the pumpkins.

The Biggest Pumpkin

Take these eleven steps to grow the biggest pumpkin in town.

1. Select seeds from a large pumpkin. Big Max (120 days) is a good choice.

2. Dig a hole as big as a bushel basket.

3. Dump in lots of compost or well-rotted manure, or a pound of a commercial fertilizer such as 10-10-10. Cover with four inches of soil.

4. Plant three seeds, covering with one inch of soil.

5. When plants have three or four leaves, snip back all but the strongest plant.

6. Keep plant weed-free and well watered.

7. When vine has produced 3 small pumpkins, snip off the fuzzy end of the vine.

8. Pick off any new blossoms or fruit.

9. When pumpkins are big-fist size, pick off the two smaller ones.

10. Roll the pumpkin over gently occasionally, so it will be round and evenly colored.

11. When it is mature, cut it from the vine, then, with the help of friends, load it into a truck and take it to the county fair.

Radishes

While radish-raising isn't as challenging as the propagation of orchids, this spicy little root deserves a place in everyone's garden as a lively harbinger of spring, enlivening the family salad and giving a tasty hint of the good the garden is about to offer. A cool weather vegetable, the radish is grown in winter in the South, the spring and fall in the North. Likes rich, sandy loam. A half-ounce of seed will yield twenty-five pounds—but should be planted in much smaller amounts, such as a two-foot section of a wide row, or mixed in with carrots and other vegetables, to be harvested long before their bedmates. Planted this way, radishes tend to keep the weeds out of the bed, making it much easier to grow crops such as carrots.

Planting: As soon as soil can be worked, sow seeds about one inch apart in rows one foot apart, or in wide rows. Cover with a quarter-inch of soil or sifted compost. Plant early varieties first, switch to summer varieties when weather warms up, then switch to late varieties.

Cultivation: In their quick growing season, radishes demand little assistance beyond weeding and watering.

Harvesting: Pick before or as they reach maturity. Leave late varieties in ground until after frost, then pull up and store in damp sand in cellar.

Enemies: To avoid maggots, plant late, or avoid planting where any member of the cabbage family has grown in the past three years.

Varieties: Cherry Belle (Twenty-two days. Early. Bright red. Round and smooth. Good eating). Sparkler (Twenty-five days. Round, red with lower portion of root white). White Icicle (Twenty-eight days. Summer. Slender roots. White skin). Celestial (Sixty days. Late variety. Six to eight inches of pure white root. Good to store).

Suggestions: Janet Ballantyne, who wrote the Joy of Gardening Cookbook, has convinced me that there are ways to cook radishes. Two of her methods are steaming whole radishes for eight minutes, then serving them with a cream or cheese sauce, and steaming sliced radishes and baby peas for two to four minutes, then topping them with an herb butter. They are also good sliced and stir-fried, much as you would use water chestnuts.

Fall Radishes

Most gardeners plant one crop of radishes in the early spring. Three weeks later they're knee-deep in radishes, and in another week, the radishes are too large to eat.

For top results, try several fall plantings, putting in a few in mid-summer, and a few more every three weeks thereafter. They'll grow fast at that time, and the problem of root maggots will be avoided.

19 ____

Planting	Variety	Date Planted	Amount Planted (Row Length)
1.			
2.			
3.			

Harvest Dates	Variety	Expected	Actual
1.			
2.			
3.			

Satisfied With Variety, Amount?

19 ____

Planting	Variety	Date Planted	Amount Planted (Row Length)
1.			
2.			
3.			

Harvest Dates	Variety	Expected	Actual
1.			
2.			
3.			

Satisfied With Variety, Amount?

19 ____

Planting	Variety	Date Planted	Amount Planted (Row Length)
1.			
2.			
3.			

Harvest Dates	Variety	Expected	Actual
1.			
2.			
3.			

Satisfied With Variety, Amount?

19 ___

Planting	Variety	Date Planted	Amount Planted (Row Length)
1.			
2.			
3.			

Harvest Dates	Variety	Expected	Actual
1.			
2.			
3.			

Satisfied With Variety, Amount?

---

19 ___

Planting	Variety	Date Planted	Amount Planted (Row Length)
1.			
2.			
3.			

Harvest Dates	Variety	Expected	Actual
1.			
2.			
3.			

Satisfied With Variety, Amount?

---

19 ___

Planting	Variety	Date Planted	Amount Planted (Row Length)
1.			
2.			
3.			

Harvest Dates	Variety	Expected	Actual
1.			
2.			
3.			

Satisfied With Variety, Amount?

Rutabaga

This member of the cabbage family is very much like the turnip, and that explains its other names—Swedish turnip, Swede turnip, winter turnip, and yellow turnip. This hardy root crop is high in food value, easy to grow, and stores well—better than turnip. An eighth of an ounce of seed will yield fifty pounds of rutabagas—more than most people want. Fine to grow in a wide row or raised bed. Moist, rich soil.

Planting: Rutabaga is best when it is sown to mature in the fall. To decide when to plant, know the days to harvest, and count back that many days from the first fall frost date. Sow seeds a quarter-inch deep in rows eighteen inches apart, or sow and thin in a wide row or raised bed to have rutabaga growing eight to twelve inches apart. Keep seedbed moist. Rutabaga doesn't do well south of the Mason-Dixon line. Sow turnips there.

Cultivation: In heat of summer, provide young plants with plenty of moisture, and mulch well.

Harvesting: About ninety days after planting, when roots are four to five inches across (much larger than turnips), grasp tops and pull up the roots. This can be after first frost, but should be done before ground is frozen, or keeping quality will suffer. Can be stored in a root cellar or pit, or buried in moist sand, in cellar, or kept in a plastic bag in the cellar or refrigerator. This root will store like a rock.

Enemies: All enemies of the cabbage family should be guarded against, but seldom will they harm this hardy plant.

Varieties: Not a large selection. Burpee's Purple Top Yellow (Ninety days to harvest. Fine-grained yellow flesh. Good keeper). American Purple Top (Ninety days. Light yellow, firm flesh). Laurentian (Ninety days. Deep purple top, smooth root, yellow flesh).

Suggestions: Begin harvesting soon after root has swollen. I've grown rutabagas as large as eleven pounds that didn't become pithy—but what do you do with eleven pounds of rutabaga?

Salsify

Also called oyster plant and vegetable oyster because of the taste of its long, thin roots when cooked—but it tastes like parsnips to me. Every gardener should try this at least once. Growth is similar to parsnips, but growing season is longer. Light mellow soil, well drained, with compost worked in deep. This is an ideal crop for a raised bed, since those long roots will appreciate the depth of the well-worked soil. Plants grow with tapering tap roots eight to ten inches in length, 1½ inches in diameter. Half-ounce of seed should produce more than 250 roots—and that's a lot of salsify. Avoid use of manure unless it is well rotted, or salsify will have hairy secondary roots.

Planting: Purchase fresh seed each year. Sow seed half-inch deep, fairly thickly, in rows twelve to fifteen inches apart, or in wide rows. When plants are three inches high, thin to stand four inches apart.

Cultivation: Keep soil moist, mulch after thinning, and remove the competition of any weeds.

Harvesting: Heavy frost improves the flavor. Dig as needed after a frost, or dig to store in root pit or root cellar, or in damp sand in cellar. However, since roots tend to shrivel and become tough when stored these ways, the preferred method is to leave the roots in the ground until needed. Be sure to harvest them before the growth begins in the spring.

Enemies: Salsify has few friends among gardeners; it has even fewer pest or disease enemies.

Varieties: Mammoth Sandwich Island (120 days. With creamy white root flesh) is usually the only available variety.

Suggestions: The salsify has a black-skinned brother called scorzonera or black salsify. It is grown, harvested, and eaten the same way as salsify, but some people prefer its flavor. Both salsify and scorzonera have a delightfully different taste.

19 ____

Planting   Variety   Date Planted   Amount Planted (Row Length)

1. _____   _____   _____

2. _____   _____   _____

3. _____   _____   _____

Harvest Dates   Variety   Expected   Actual

1. _____   _____   _____

2. _____   _____   _____

3. _____   _____   _____

Satisfied With Variety, Amount? _____

_____

19 ____

Planting   Variety   Date Planted   Amount Planted (Row Length)

1. _____   _____   _____

2. _____   _____   _____

3. _____   _____   _____

Harvest Dates   Variety   Expected   Actual

1. _____   _____   _____

2. _____   _____   _____

3. _____   _____   _____

Satisfied With Variety, Amount? _____

_____

19 ____

Planting   Variety   Date Planted   Amount Planted (Row Length)

1. _____   _____   _____

2. _____   _____   _____

3. _____   _____   _____

Harvest Dates   Variety   Expected   Actual

1. _____   _____   _____

2. _____   _____   _____

3. _____   _____   _____

Satisfied With Variety, Amount? _____

_____

19 ____

Planting	Variety	Date Planted	Amount Planted (Row Length)
1.			
2.			
3.			

Harvest Dates	Variety	Expected	Actual
1.			
2.			
3.			

Satisfied With Variety, Amount?

_____

_____

19 ____

Planting	Variety	Date Planted	Amount Planted (Row Length)
1.			
2.			
3.			

Harvest Dates	Variety	Expected	Actual
1.			
2.			
3.			

Satisfied With Variety, Amount?

_____

_____

19 ____

Planting	Variety	Date Planted	Amount Planted (Row Length)
1.			
2.			
3.			

Harvest Dates	Variety	Expected	Actual
1.			
2.			
3.			

Satisfied With Variety, Amount?

_____

_____

Soybeans

Soybeans have a lot going for them. They're stuffed with proteins, easy to grow, and can be eaten as shell beans, green or dried. I have just one criticism of them: I've never found a variety I liked to eat. Slower growing than other bush beans. Yield per unit of land is so small that only those with large gardening areas should consider growing them. Five to six ounces of seed will yield fifteen pounds of pods, half of that amount of beans. Good in a wide row, and they're excellent for a green manure crop.

Planting: Dust seeds with a nitrogen inoculant made especially for soybeans. Two weeks after last spring frost, plant seeds one inch deep, two inches apart in rows two to three feet apart. Thin plants to three to four inches apart. Require fertile, well-drained, mellow soil with additional lime.

Cultivation: Shallow root system, so avoid deep cultivation. Can be mulched when four inches tall.

Harvesting: For use as green beans, harvest pods when beans are fully grown but before pods turn yellow. Use like limas. Harvest period is seven to ten days. Steam or parboil pods four to five minutes, in small batches, before attempting to shell them. To get dry soybeans, pick when beans are dry but stems are still green. Otherwise, if picking is delayed, pods will break, scattering beans. Dried beans can be baked or sprouted.

Enemies: Soybeans are a favorite of rabbits and chipmunks. Diseases such as brown spot, bacterial blight, and downy mildew can be avoided by rotating the crop with other crops, and composting the vines at the end of the season.

Varieties: Kanrich (103 days to matuity. Bushes are twenty-four inches high. Pods contain two or three beans. When green, can be eaten as shell beans; when mature and dried, may be cooked similarly to lima beans). Fiskby V (Seventy days. Bushes are fourteen inches high, and upright. Good in northern areas. Frost Beater (Seventy-five days. Extra early-maturing variety).

Spinach

This is a cool-weather crop to be planted as soon as soil can be worked, then raised quickly and harvested before it goes to seed. Grown in winter in South, in early spring and late fall in North. Will grow on any fertile soil, with plenty of nitrogen. Lime should be added if soil is at all acid. Half-ounce of seed will yield forty pounds of spinach.

Planting: A good wide-row crop, since it will shade the soil, keep it cool, and thus delay the process of going to seed that makes plant inedible. Plant fresh seeds each year, as soon as ground can be worked. In a row the width of a garden rake, have plants three to four inches apart. In narrow rows, have plants three or four inches apart, rows twelve inches apart. Successive plantings are recommended, stopping in mid-summer, but resuming for fall harvest.

Cultivation: Little needs to be done with a wide row. For narrow rows, mulch to keep soil cooler.

Harvesting: Harvest early, when plants are small, then eat the leaves raw, in a spinach salad. Cut plants low, but leave the tiny center leaves to grow, then cut it again when it has four to six leaves. Cut a lot each time—spinach cooks down alarmingly. Good frozen.

Enemies: Plant blight-resistant varieties, keep well weeded or heavily mulched, and remain ignorant of the diseases listed for this vegetable. Hand pick if you see any of the spinach flea beetles, quarter-inch, greenish-black fellows, or their larvae, both found on the undersides of leaves.

Varieties: Melody (Forty-two days. My favorite. A vigorous plant with semi-crinkled leaves). Bloomsdale Long Standing (Forty-eight days. Savoyed. Resists bolting). Early Hybrid #7 (Forty-two days. Resistant to downy mildew. Semi-savoyed leaves. Good for freezing and canning).

Suggestions: In most northern climates you can plant spinach in early fall and it will overwinter and grow in spring, if it is protected by a good snow cover.

19 ____

Planting	Variety	Date Planted	Amount Planted (Row Length)
1.			
2.			
3.			

Harvest Dates	Variety	Expected	Actual
1.			
2.			
3.			

Satisfied With Variety, Amount?

19 ____

Planting	Variety	Date Planted	Amount Planted (Row Length)
1.			
2.			
3.			

Harvest Dates	Variety	Expected	Actual
1.			
2.			
3.			

Satisfied With Variety, Amount?

19 ____

Planting	Variety	Date Planted	Amount Planted (Row Length)
1.			
2.			
3.			

Harvest Dates	Variety	Expected	Actual
1.			
2.			
3.			

Satisfied With Variety, Amount?

19 ____

Planting	Variety	Date Planted	Amount Planted (Row Length)
1.			
2.			
3.			

Harvest Dates	Variety	Expected	Actual
1.			
2.			
3.			

Satisfied With Variety, Amount?

19 ____

Planting	Variety	Date Planted	Amount Planted (Row Length)
1.			
2.			
3.			

Harvest Dates	Variety	Expected	Actual
1.			
2.			
3.			

Satisfied With Variety, Amount?

19 ____

Planting	Variety	Date Planted	Amount Planted (Row Length)
1.			
2.			
3.			

Harvest Dates	Variety	Expected	Actual
1.			
2.			
3.			

Satisfied With Variety, Amount?

Squash, Summer

Prizes should be awarded to gardeners who grow no more summer squash than they can eat. There's a huge variety to choose from, so restraint in planting is essential. A truly American plant, squash grows throughout the United States, and in abundance. A quarter-pound of seeds will yield at least 150 squash. Bush varieties yield more in less space. All like a deep, rich soil. If cool climates are a problem, grow on a raised bed.

Planting: Spade well-rotted manure or compost into sandy loam. Most folks won't need to plant any more than five feet of each variety. Allow four feet between rows. When danger of frost is past, soil is warm, plant seeds half-inch deep and six inches apart.

Cultivation: Keep weeded and well watered. Side-dress when buds appear.

Harvesting: Pick early and often. Summer squash is best before it matures, and is still tender and tasty. To keep crop growing, pick any large squash and add them to the compost pile.

Enemies: If given a good start, plants will nearly care for themselves. Use fresh seed, add compost to hills, and rotate crops. Rotenone will discourage the squash bug and the cucumber beetle, striped and spotted. Squash bugs will hide under shingles and boards, and can be uncovered and killed early in the morning. Radishes, too, will attract them. If cucumber beetles are a problem, start plants indoors, or protect plants with a tent of cheesecloth. Squash vine borer is present if mature vine suddenly wilts. Using a sharp knife, slit vine back to where white grub, the borer, will be found. Get rid of him, then cover slit stem with soil, giving it a chance to form roots. If desperate, apply Sevin for all these enemies.

Varieties: There are more good ones than can be listed, so read seed catalogs and experiment. Early Prolific Straightneck (Fifty days. Bush. Good for all uses. Creamy yellow fruit good from four to six inches until they are twelve to fourteen inches long). White Bush Patty Pan (Fifty-four days. Bush. Deliciously mild). Zucchini (Fifty days. Bush. Very prolific).

Suggestions: Harvest summer squash when they're small, and try them raw, with slices used as a base for canapes, topped with various dips and spreads. I never cared for Patty Pan until a fellow gardener suggested harvesting them before the squash were two inches in diameter, half-dollar size is even better, then served with a little butter and salt and pepper... delicious.

An Early Squash Treat

You don't have to wait until squash matures to enjoy a harvest from those squash vines.

Pick a quantity of buds, just before they're ready to pop open into blossoms. Rinse them off, then saute them in butter. You'll find they add a lot to soups and stews, or served with meat.

And don't worry about cutting down on your harvest of squash. The vines will simply produce more buds.

Squash, Winter

Select several varieties and be prepared to sacrifice a lot of space unless you choose the bush varieties. Grown throughout the United States, each area having its favorites. Plant squash in sandy loam, adding plenty of compost or well-rotted manure. Half-ounce of seed in hills will yield seventy-five or far more pounds of squash, depending on the variety.

Planting: If garden is adjacent to uncultivated area, plant squash so vines can rampage out of garden, rather than across rows of carefully cultivated crops. Plant in rows spaced eight to ten feet apart. Bush varieties can be closer, five or six feet apart. After all danger of frost is past, set seeds five to six inches apart and one inch deep. Can be started indoors in peat pots a month in advance, but care must be taken to avoid damaging tap root when transplanting.

Cultivation: Keep soil moist. When bush squash have set six fruit, thin off any extra, for best quality.

Harvesting: Unlike summer squash, winter types must mature fully on the vine, attaining full growth and hardened skins, for best storage characteristics. Before first frost, cut squash off vine with a sharp knife. Handle gently, let cure in warm, airy, sheltered location, then store all sound fruit in dry cellar, with temperatures between 40° and 50°.

Enemies: Same as for summer squash.

Varieties: Experiment with several, particularly the space-saving bush varieties, to find the ones you like best. Try these: Butternut (Eighty-five days. Tops on the list for flavor. Good keeper and resistant to the squash borer). Blue Hubbard (120 days. A traditional variety, with impressive fifteen-pounders not at all uncommon. Good keeper and tasty). Gold Nugget (Eighty-five days. Bush type. Requires little room. Small pumpkin-shaped. Bright orange fruit with deep yellow flesh. Good baked in shell). Table Queen or Acorn (Eighty days. Good baked in shell, with half making a serving. A favorite of most housewives).

Suggestions: Try New Jersey Golden Acorn. This squash can be eaten as a summer squash when immature, or allowed to mature for winter squash. Very tasty. One drawback is that it doesn't keep as well as others, so eat it up in late fall and early winter. Semi-bush habit. Grows well on fences or trellises to save space.

Testing Winter Squash

Give your winter squash the thumbnail test before storing them.

Push a thumbnail against the skin. If it doesn't cut easily, that squash will keep for a long time. But if your nail slides quite easily into the skin, eat that squash in the fall, or it will spoil.

19 _____

Planting	Variety	Date Planted	Amount Planted (Row Length)
1.	_____	_____	_____
2.	_____	_____	_____
3.	_____	_____	_____

Harvest Dates	Variety	Expected	Actual
1.	_____	_____	_____
2.	_____	_____	_____
3.	_____	_____	_____

Satisfied With Variety, Amount? _____

_____

19 _____

Planting	Variety	Date Planted	Amount Planted (Row Length)
1.	_____	_____	_____
2.	_____	_____	_____
3.	_____	_____	_____

Harvest Dates	Variety	Expected	Actual
1.	_____	_____	_____
2.	_____	_____	_____
3.	_____	_____	_____

Satisfied With Variety, Amount? _____

_____

19 _____

Planting	Variety	Date Planted	Amount Planted (Row Length)
1.	_____	_____	_____
2.	_____	_____	_____
3.	_____	_____	_____

Harvest Dates	Variety	Expected	Actual
1.	_____	_____	_____
2.	_____	_____	_____
3.	_____	_____	_____

Satisfied With Variety, Amount? _____

_____

19 ____

Planting | Variety | Date Planted | Amount Planted (Row Length)

1. _____ _____ _____
2. _____ _____ _____
3. _____ _____ _____

Harvest Dates | Variety | Expected | Actual

1. _____ _____ _____
2. _____ _____ _____
3. _____ _____ _____

Satisfied With Variety, Amount? _____

_____

19 ____

Planting | Variety | Date Planted | Amount Planted (Row Length)

1. _____ _____ _____
2. _____ _____ _____
3. _____ _____ _____

Harvest Dates | Variety | Expected | Actual

1. _____ _____ _____
2. _____ _____ _____
3. _____ _____ _____

Satisfied With Variety, Amount? _____

_____

19 ____

Planting | Variety | Date Planted | Amount Planted (Row Length)

1. _____ _____ _____
2. _____ _____ _____
3. _____ _____ _____

Harvest Dates | Variety | Expected | Actual

1. _____ _____ _____
2. _____ _____ _____
3. _____ _____ _____

Satisfied With Variety, Amount? _____

_____

Sweet Potatoes

Traditionally a Southern crop, but can be grown in any location that is frost-free for 100 days. Prefers light, sandy soil that is well drained. Fifty slips planted in a fifty-foot row will yield fifty pounds of potatoes. Good for raised beds.

Planting: Except in Deep South, sweet potatoes are started indoors, to stretch season enough for a good crop. They are started from slips, purchased, or grown by gardener. To start slips, begin two months before night temperatures will remain above 60°. In a hotbed or indoors, lay sweet potatoes on their sides and cover with two inches of moist sand. Get temperature up to 75°-80°. Sprout slips six to nine inches long will develop in six to seven weeks. These may be broken off with a twisting tug. In garden, form a ridge eight to ten inches high. Set slips a foot apart on top of the ridge, and press four inches of each slip into the soil. Water to settle the slip. Space rows three feet apart. Slips do not need roots to grow.

Cultivation: Keep weed-free until thick vines take over this job. Water well until vines begin to spread. After that the roots will be deep enough to find the moisture the plants require.

Harvesting: Dig them before first frost, when the foliage begins to turn yellow, and preferably when the soil is fairly dry. Use spading fork carefully, to avoid bruising them. Eat damaged potatoes first. Let those harvested dry two to three hours in field, then cure them for 10 days in 85° temperature. Gradually reduce temperature to 50°-55° for storage. In South, gardeners time planting to harvest by late September and early October.

Enemies: The sweet potato weevil and the sweet potato beetle are the most common pests. The larvae of the weevils eat down the plants into the potatoes, ruining them. The weevils do not hibernate. Remove their food supply by disposing of crop residues after harvest.

Varieties: Ask gardeners in your area which varieties grow best there. Centennial (100 days. Moist variety. Do best in cool climates. Good yield). Porto Rico (150 days. Bush type. Deep orange flesh). Jersey Orange (150 days. Dry-fleshed variety).

Suggestions: Southern gardeners, with long growing seasons, will have no trouble growing full-size sweet potatoes; in fact, they can grow them far larger than are wanted. Northern gardeners, enjoying cooler, shorter seasons, can console themselves by remembering that even smaller sweet potatoes taste just as good as the larger ones. I always grow some sweet potatoes. The plants are beautiful, the taste of sweet potatoes is delicious, and they're easy to grow. If you've never tried them, you don't know what you're missing.

Swiss Chard

One of my favorite greens. I prefer the red varieties. I think they taste better, but it may be purely psychological, since I enjoy seeing the red chard growing. An excellent garden crop since it sends down long, powerful roots that will break up heavy subsoil. Mellow soil, not acid, should be enriched for best crop. Only a single planting is required. Quarter-ounce of seed sparsely sown will yield fifty or more pounds of chard. A good fall crop, and an excellent crop to raise in a wide row or on a raised bed.

Planting: As soon as ground can be prepared, plant seeds two or three inches apart in a wide row or on a raised bed and thin to four to six inches apart, or in a narrow row with plants three to four inches apart and rows eighteen inches apart. Plant seeds one inch deep. In the South, plant in the fall and harvest all winter.

Harvesting: When plants are six inches tall, thin by removing every other plant (and using them in the kitchen). When remaining plants reach six or seven inches high, harvest by cutting back to one inch above the ground. Plants will grow again, and you'll get three to four harvests. In late summer, cut back all plants, and side-dress crop, for a harvest that will last until early winter.

Enemies: Mexican bean beetles can be hand picked, and their eggs on the underside of leaves should be crushed. I find that goldfinches love this crop.

Varieties: Fordhook Giant (Sixty days to first cutting. Emerald green with white stalks. Heavily crumpled leaves). Ruby (Sixty days. A beautiful, bright crimson rhubarb chard, with sweet flavor).

Suggestions: If you have trouble raising spinach, or tire of seeing it suddenly go to seed with the first hot spell, try Swiss chard as a substitute. It's easy to grow, can be harvested for a long season, and I like its taste as well as that of spinach. Another good point is that it doesn't cook down the way spinach will.

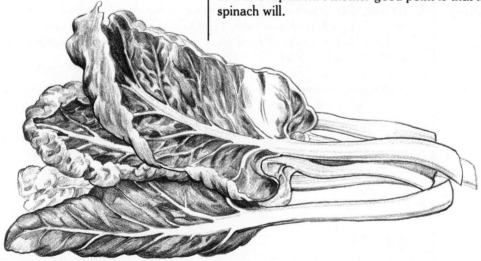

19 _____

Planting	Variety	Date Planted	Amount Planted (Row Length)
1.	_____	_____	_____
2.	_____	_____	_____
3.	_____	_____	_____

Harvest Dates	Variety	Expected	Actual
1.	_____	_____	_____
2.	_____	_____	_____
3.	_____	_____	_____

Satisfied With Variety, Amount? _____

_____

19 _____

Planting	Variety	Date Planted	Amount Planted (Row Length)
1.	_____	_____	_____
2.	_____	_____	_____
3.	_____	_____	_____

Harvest Dates	Variety	Expected	Actual
1.	_____	_____	_____
2.	_____	_____	_____
3.	_____	_____	_____

Satisfied With Variety, Amount? _____

_____

19 _____

Planting	Variety	Date Planted	Amount Planted (Row Length)
1.	_____	_____	_____
2.	_____	_____	_____
3.	_____	_____	_____

Harvest Dates	Variety	Expected	Actual
1.	_____	_____	_____
2.	_____	_____	_____
3.	_____	_____	_____

Satisfied With Variety, Amount? _____

_____

19 ____

Planting	Variety	Date Planted	Amount Planted (Row Length)
1.			
2.			
3.			

Harvest Dates	Variety	Expected	Actual
1.			
2.			
3.			

Satisfied With Variety, Amount?

---

19 ____

Planting	Variety	Date Planted	Amount Planted (Row Length)
1.			
2.			
3.			

Harvest Dates	Variety	Expected	Actual
1.			
2.			
3.			

Satisfied With Variety, Amount?

---

19 ____

Planting	Variety	Date Planted	Amount Planted (Row Length)
1.			
2.			
3.			

Harvest Dates	Variety	Expected	Actual
1.			
2.			
3.			

Satisfied With Variety, Amount?

Tomatoes

A must crop in every garden, no matter how small that garden is. Experiment with different varieties each year. Tomatoes grow throughout the United States, in winter in the extreme South, and in the spring, summer, and fall further north. Just ten plants can yield 100 pounds of tomatoes. Sprawling tomato plants will produce more tomatoes, of lesser quality, and may attract slugs. If you have soil problems, such as clay soil or wet soil, try a raised bed for your tomatoes.

Planting: Most of us start our tomato plants far too early, and have leggy plants when it's time to transplant them. The best transplants are no more than eight weeks old, or eight inches high. A common method is to start them in flats, in 70°-75° temperatures, in an artificial soil mix. Transplant them to three-inch peat pots, and set them deep in the pots, when they have true leaves. Keep them under fluorescent lights, in temperatures of about 65°. Harden them off by putting them outside for the ten days before you transplant them, giving them more sunlight every day. Set out on a cloudy day when danger of frost is past, setting them deep so additional roots can grow along the stem. If you plan to stake them, put the stake in at this time. Plant three feet apart in rows four feet apart if sprawling, or two feet apart in rows three feet apart if staked. Use same distances for tomatoes in wire cages.

Cultivation: Mulch heavily when soil is warm, about time plants blossom. Until then, cultivate to keep weeds down, and provide moisture. Remove suckers that grow between branches.

Harvesting: Let tomatoes ripen on vine for best eating. Keep them picked. When frost threatens, pick green tomatoes, put them on a shelf, and cover with sheets of newspaper. Check daily to use ripened tomatoes.

Enemies: Place newspaper collars around young plants when setting out, to defeat cutworms. Search out and destroy the huge green tomato worm, or control it with BT. Many diseases can be avoided by planting resistant varieties, giving plants ample room, providing plenty of humus and moisture, and not working in them when plants are wet.

Varieties: Select tomatoes for specific uses, such as Better Boy (Seventy days) as the main crop, Red Cherry (Seventy-two days) or Yellow Pear (Seventy days) for salads, Roma VF (Seventy-two days) for paste and sauce.

Suggestions: To get early tomatoes, start an early variety (Pixie, Coldset, or Early Girl) eight to twelve weeks before last frost. Set them out three to four weeks before last frost. Enclose each in a wire cylinder covered with clear plastic to trap heat. If frosts threaten, cover with newspaper sheets right in cylinder.

Tomatoes grown in a window tend to get too leggy and lean toward the window. Turn them daily and they will grow stems that are shorter and thicker. It's better to grow them under fluorescent lights.

Turnip

This cool-weather crop is raised for both its roots and its tops. Turnips are usually grown as a summer crop in the North, and planted in July and August; in the South, they're planted in February and March, then new plantings, just for the greens, are started from July through October. Like moist, rich soil, but not too heavy with nitrogen. A quarter-ounce of seed row will yield fifty pounds. A good wide-row crop.

Planting: Sow seed a quarter-inch deep, very sparsely, in wide rows or in rows eighteen inches apart. Moisten with a spray.

Cultivation: In a raised bed, thin to three to five inches apart. In single row, keep turnips same distance apart.

Harvesting: When thinning, use thinnings as greens. Early crop may be harvested when roots are 1½ inches in diameter. Harvest fall crop after first frost. Cut off tops, close and store in root cellar, where it is cool and damp. Turnips don't store as well as rutabagas.

Enemies: If cabbage worms show interest, see under Broccoli for sure-fire method of destroying them.

Varieties: Purple-Top White Globe (Fifty-five days. So crisp and tasty it can be eaten raw. Harvest when two to three inches in diameter). Purple-Top Milan (Forty-five days. Try this for a spring crop). Shogoin (Thirty days to greens, seventy days for roots. Delicious). Tokyo Cross (Forty-five days. White. Excellent for greens).

Suggestions: While turnips do best when grown as a fall crop, try a spring crop, planting when soil can be worked. It's a way to get an early crop of delicious greens and tender roots.

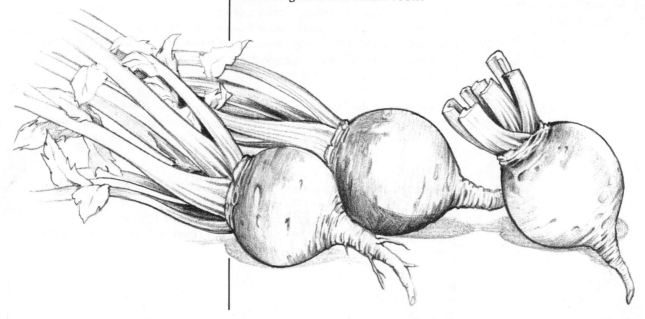

19 ____

Planting	Variety	Date Planted	Amount Planted (Row Length)
1.			
2.			
3.			

Harvest Dates	Variety	Expected	Actual
1.			
2.			
3.			

Satisfied With Variety, Amount?

19 ____

Planting	Variety	Date Planted	Amount Planted (Row Length)
1.			
2.			
3.			

Harvest Dates	Variety	Expected	Actual
1.			
2.			
3.			

Satisfied With Variety, Amount?

19 ____

Planting	Variety	Date Planted	Amount Planted (Row Length)
1.			
2.			
3.			

Harvest Dates	Variety	Expected	Actual
1.			
2.			
3.			

Satisfied With Variety, Amount?

19 ____

Planting	Variety	Date Planted	Amount Planted (Row Length)
1.			
2.			
3.			

Harvest Dates	Variety	Expected	Actual
1.			
2.			
3.			

Satisfied With Variety, Amount?

_____

_____

19 ____

Planting	Variety	Date Planted	Amount Planted (Row Length)
1.			
2.			
3.			

Harvest Dates	Variety	Expected	Actual
1.			
2.			
3.			

Satisfied With Variety, Amount?

_____

_____

19 ____

Planting	Variety	Date Planted	Amount Planted (Row Length)
1.			
2.			
3.			

Harvest Dates	Variety	Expected	Actual
1.			
2.			
3.			

Satisfied With Variety, Amount?

_____

_____

Watermelon

Originally a tropical African plant, watermelon was grown for decades in the South, to the envy of northern gardeners. But now watermelons that will reach maturity in a short season have been developed, so crop is common through much of the country. Gardeners should note it takes some thirty-six square feet to produce four watermelons. Sandy, slightly acid soil with a lot of humus needed. The plant wants moisture at all times. Packet of seeds will produce twenty-five to thirty watermelons.

Planting: For a good crop, provide loose, rich soil, lots of moisture—and warm weather. A minimum of three months of frost-free weather is needed for larger varieties, but smaller ones can be grown in less time. Plant when all danger of frost is past. To lengthen growing season in North, start plants indoors six to eight weeks in advance of garden-planting time. Place three seeds half-inch deep in soil in three-inch pots. Thin to one per pot by clipping off all but the strongest vine. Plant pots a foot apart. If planting seeds, place seeds half-inch deep and two to three inches apart. Rows with both pots and seeds should be six to eight feet apart. Protect young plants with hot caps or plastic tunnels.

Cultivation: Hoe discreetly for several weeks to keep weeds down. To speed development of fruit, many growers limit to two the number of watermelons per vine. Late-set fruit should be removed.

Harvesting: Fruits must ripen on the vine. Judging when they should be picked requires practice. Lighter areas of melon should turn to creamy white. Experts judge by sound made when knuckles are rapped on melon. The green melon "pings" while the ripe melon "thuds."

Enemies: Avoid most of them by crop rotation, planting resistant varieties. Cucumber beetles will attack vines. Hot caps can be used to protect young vines.

Varieties: Find out what varieties do best in your area. New Hampshire Midget (Sixty-eight days. The one to try in the North when you've been told you can't grow watermelon. Five- or six-inch fruit with thin rind and good flavor). Sugar Baby (Seventy-five days. Larger than N.H. Midget. Sweet variety). Dixie Queen (Ninety days. A round, striped green melon. Wilt resistant. Crisp, sweet flesh). Yellow Doll (Seventy-five days. Crisp, yellow flesh. Few seeds). Two other favorites are Charleston Grey (Eighty-five to ninety days) and Kleckley Sweet (Eighty-seven days).

Suggestions: For an impressive melon in the South, try State Fair, which grow to 50-100 pounds of firm sweet flesh, or Week's Giant Watermelon, the record-large melon at 197 pounds.

Asparagus

An asparagus bed is a must for the gourmet gardener. It's a lot of work to establish a bed, but well worth it. Grows well throughout United States as far south as southern Georgia. Thirty-five roots in a fifty-foot bed will yield about fifteen pounds.

Planting: For planting roots, select a garden site in a section where the bed will not interfere with annual crops. In early spring, or in fall in the South, dig a trench twelve to fourteen inches deep and ten inches wide. In the bottom, dig in a six-inch layer of compost and rotted manure, plus lime if needed, plus a dusting of 10-10-10 fertilizer. Build small mounds eighteen inches apart in the bottom of the trench, then set each two-year-old crown on top of a mound, and drape the roots around it. Cover with two inches of soil. As the shoots grow, gradually fill in the trench.

Cultivation: The first year, mulch heavily after spears appear and begin to fern, to hold moisture and discourage weeds. Second year, and thereafter, in early spring, before growth starts, cut old ferns and remove the mulch. Fertilize with a cupful of 10-10-10 for each three feet of row, or use a rich compost. After harvesting, weed carefully, then mulch around the growing spears to keep down weeds.

Harvesting: Don't harvest the year of planting, and harvest lightly the year after; then, in third year, harvest when spears reach four to eight inches. Cut spears just below the surface of the soil. You can harvest for five to eight weeks each spring, then allow shoots to grow throughout summer.

Enemies: Beetles attracted to asparagus can be hand picked or sprayed with malathion or Sevin. Asparagus rust can be avoided with rust-resistant varieties.

Varieties: In early part of this century, rust threatened the entire commercial crop, and resulted in an intensive development program. The result was Mary Washington (Most widely grown, good fresh, canned, or frozen), Martha Washington, and, later, Viking (or Mary Washington Improved, widely grown in the Midwest), all rust-resistant.

Suggestions: If you can wait another year for harvesting asparagus, try planting seeds. Select a well-drained, sandy loam, and plant seeds one inch deep and an inch apart, later thinning to three inches apart. Seeds are very slow to germinate, so it's well to mark site with radishes. The following spring, dig up the roots and plant them in a permanent bed, prepared as described above. Weeds are the big problem, so be sure to keep this nursery well weeded.

ASPARAGUS HARVEST

Date Bed Started: _____

Variety: _____

Number of Roots, and Where Obtained: _____

Details of Planting (depth of trench, width, amount of compost, fertilizer, etc): _____
_____
_____

Do not harvest first year after starting bed; harvest lightly second year.

Second Year 19 ___		Third Year 19 ___		Fourth Year 19 ___	
Date	Amount	Date	Amount	Date	Amount
TOTAL _____		TOTAL _____		TOTAL _____	

Notes: _____
_____
_____
_____
_____

HORSERADISH HARVEST

Date Planted: _____

Variety: _____

Number of Roots, and Where Obtained: _____

Details of Planting: _____

_____

_____

Amounts Harvested

First Year		Second Year		Third Year	
Date	Amount	Date	Amount	Date	Amount

How Prepared and How Liked

First Year: _____

_____

_____

Second Year: _____

_____

_____

Third Year: _____

_____

_____

Notes: _____

_____

_____

_____

_____

_____

_____

Horseradish

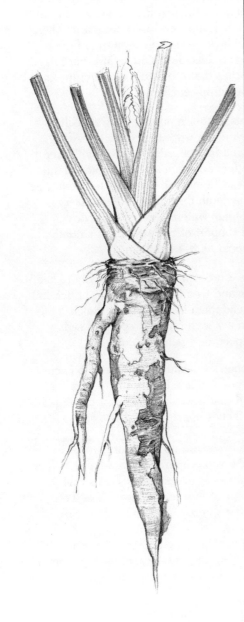

This perennial is grown in temperate regions where soil freezes in the winter. It is grown for its thick, white roots, which are ground and used as a condiment. It prefers rich, loose soil, deeply prepared so roots grow long and straight. Only a few plants are needed to start a bed. Horseradish tends to spread, so care should be used in selecting a site.

Planting: Buy, or get from a neighbor, six root cuttings, three to four inches long and middle-finger thick. Dig a six-inch deep trench, then plant the roots a foot apart, at a 45° angle, top side up, and cover with two inches of soil.

Cultivation: When plants are up, mulch to eliminate competition from weeds.

Harvesting: Best harvested in early spring, before growth starts, or late fall, although it can be harvested at any time. Dig roots as needed. It's almost impossible to harvest so much that the bed is depleted, since pieces of root will grow again.

Enemies: Few insects will tackle this husky herb. The occasional flea beetle that invades the foliage can be discouraged with rotenone, but usually isn't necessary.

Varieties: While most gardeners grow horseradish of unknown parentage, seed catalogs list two varieties, Bohemian Horseradish, with its large, white roots, and Maliner Kren.

Suggestions: To make prepared horseradish, wash and peel the roots, and chop them into small pieces. Add three to four tablespoons of water and one to two tablespoons of white vinegar per cup of horseradish, then process in a blender or a food processor to the texture desired. Be careful: the aroma of this during processing can be overwhelming. The prepared horseradish can be stored in capped jars in the refrigerator for months, gradually losing its bite.

For a tangy salad dressing, mix four teaspoons of the prepared horseradish with four tablespoons cream, ¾ cup of yogurt or sour cream, and salt to taste. Serve with a green salad or chilled vegetables.

Washed horseradish roots can be stored in small quantities in your freezer. Grind it as needed for that just-picked flavor that will make your eyes water.

Raspberries

One of the earliest berries to grow, requiring little work after planting, but one of the most expensive to buy, because the fragile berries don't transport well. Delicious fresh or frozen, in shortcakes, pies, and jams. The most difficult part of raising raspberries is waiting for the first luscious crop. Try at least 20 plants for a family, and figure on about one quart per plant. There are many varieties of raspberries: red, black, yellow, even purple. I prefer the traditional red varieties, but they're **all** delicious. You've also got to choose between "summer" types (varieties that produce a single crop) and "everbearing" (raspberries that bear two crops each year).

Planting: Start with disease-free plants from a reputable grower. Gift plants often are not. Plant as soon as you can work the soil in the spring. Soil should be rich, well tilled, sandy, and free of grass and weeds. Space plants 2-3 feet apart in rows at least 6 feet apart. Soak bare-rooted plants in water for an hour or so, then trim ¼ to ½ inch off the roots to encourage new root development. Set plants at the depth they grew in the nursery or slightly deeper. Water heavily and continue watering every other day if there is no rain. Taller plants will need support of two strands of smooth wire, 30 inches apart. The top wire should be 3-4 feet high.

Cultivation: Grass and weeds can be a problem, so mulch heavily to keep them out. Weed-free mulches like bark and wood chips work fine. Each fall I use loads of shredded leaves and spread them into an 8-inch mulch around the raspberries. This packs into a 2-inch layer by spring. Feed annually with rotted manure, rich compost, or a general fertilizer.

Pruning: Remember, "summer" raspberries produce just one crop each year, on canes that grew the previous year. In late fall, prune to remove canes that have borne fruit and canes that are weak, spindly, or damaged. Stout, healthy canes should stand 6-8 inches apart within the row; prune to about 4 feet.

"Everbearing" varieties can produce two crops annually or can be pruned to produce a single fall crop. The two-crop method produces its first fruit during the summer, down on the canes of the previous year's fruiting wood. The second crop comes on the tips of this year's new canes. To prune, remove canes that bore fruit in the summer and trim fall-bearing canes to 3-4 feet following the harvest.

By cutting all the everbearing canes right to the ground each spring before their growth starts, I encourage them to produce a single big crop in the fall. I prefer this method because it's so easy and so productive.

Harvesting: Pick daily. Use small containers and don't pile berries too deeply or handle them excessively, or they will get crushed.

Enemies: Virus diseases are worst, since there are no cures for them. Leaf curl, mosaic, or orange rust are three of these. Cane borer causes tops of plants to wilt. Cut off plant 2-3 inches below wilt, and burn to kill larva that caused wilt.

Varieties: Find out from your Extension Service agent which varieties are best in your area.

RASPBERRY HARVEST

Date Set Out: _____

Variety, and Number of Each: _____

Where Obtained: _____

Details of Bed Preparation, Planting, Mulching: _____

_____

_____

Amounts Harvested

First Year			Second Year			Third Year		
Variety	Amount	Date	Variety	Amount	Date	Variety	Amount	Date

Results
Which Varieties Are Best?

First Year: _____

Second Year: _____

Third Year: _____

In space below, sketch layout of plants, by variety, in your garden.

RHUBARB HARVEST

Date Planted: _____

Variety: _____

Number of Crowns, and Where Obtained: _____
_____

Details of Bed Preparation, Planting: _____
_____
_____

Amounts Harvested

First Year		Second Year		Third Year	
Date	Amount	Date	Amount	Date	Amount

Notes: _____
_____
_____
_____
_____
_____
_____
_____
_____
_____
_____
_____
_____
_____
_____

Rhubarb

Hardy perennial grown for its tasty stalks. The leaves are poisonous. Can be grown throughout United States, but does not do well in Florida or on West Coast, since it needs a period of dormancy that comes when ground is frozen at least several inches deep. Rich, sandy, slightly acid soil. Select site carefully for your plants, since this plant will grow for years in the same location. Each mature plant will yield six to eight pounds of stalks during the six-week harvesting season in the spring. Red-stemmed and green-stemmed varieties.

Planting: Prepare hills three feet apart by digging in a quantity of leaf mold, rotted manure, or compost. Success or failure can depend on how well you do this. Crowns (also commonly called roots) should be set in soil deep enough so that the tops are four inches below the surface. Firm soil around and over them. Planting can be either in the spring or the fall.

Cultivation: Mulch heavily. Oak leaves are a good mulch. Feed each year with a layer of compost, after harvesting or in fall. If it's dry, wet thoroughly, especially when large leaves are forming. Cut back flower stalks as they develop, to conserve strength of the plant. Each four or five years, when stalks become small, dig up and divide the large clumps of roots, replanting them as described above. They can be cut in two with a spade or knife.

Harvesting: Don't for two years after planting. Third spring plants are in ground, harvest stalks with largest leaves, pulling and twisting stems from base, rather than cutting them. Leaves are a good addition to the compost pile. Do not strip plants. Take stalks at least one inch thick and ten inches long. Leave short and thin stalks to feed roots for the following year. After six weeks of intermittent harvesting, stop.

Enemies: Few enemies are strong enough to hamper the growth of this plant if it is kept fed and mulched.

Varieties: McDonalds' (Grows well in most of country. Brilliant red stalks impart a pleasingly pink tone to sauces and pies. Does not have to be peeled). Valentine (Deep red, lengthy and thick stalks). Cherry Red (Grown in milder climates, such as on West Coast).

Suggestions: Late in November, or after severe frosts, divide a few roots, leaving half of each in the ground. Put other halves in containers with peat moss and store where it is cold and dark. Late in January, move them to where the temperature is about 50° and water them. Keep them in the dark, under a cardboard box or trash can. Because there's no light, the stalks quickly grow long, tender, and leafless. I prefer the flavor of this forced rhubarb to that grown in the garden.

Strawberries

Grown throughout the United States and a favorite everywhere. Site should have rich loam, and is ideal if it slopes slightly to the south so that water will not settle on it and it warms up early in the spring. Try raised beds if drainage or heavy soil is a problem. If soil isn't rich, add ten pounds of 5-10-5 per 1,000 square feet.

Planting: Plant early in spring. Trim plant roots to four to five inches. Make small dome every eighteen inches. Place crown of plant at top of dome, spread roots around it. Add soil up to the base of the crown, firm it, and water well, preferably with a starter solution. Keep rows four feet apart.

Cultivation: Weeds ruin most strawberry beds. Mulch with straw, marsh hay, or pine needles to keep weeds down. Let plants set two to six runners, and pick off the rest. Remove all blossoms the first year, too. After first heavy freeze, mulch over entire bed. Remove this in spring as plants begin new leaf growth. Leave some to reduce weeds, and just in case there's a late frost.

Enemies: Few problems. Most insects can be controlled with Malathion.

Varieties: There are many to choose from. Select from those that do well in your area. Ask Extension Service agent or gardeners with strawberry beds.

Suggestions: If you try everbearing varieties, pick off all the blossoms in June and July, and in August you will have a good crop of berries when all others have given up. I've had best luck with Ozark Beauties. They have the classic strawberry flavor, are tender and juicy. They'll never be a good commercial crop, because they don't ship or store well, but they're ideal for the home garden.

With any variety, mulch over winter. This protects the crowns from freezing.

To defeat weeds, the enemy of the strawberry bed, beat them the year before you set out your strawberry plants. Plant an early crop of buckwheat, three pounds per thousand square feet. Till it under after about six weeks, and no later than when blossoms are seen. Plant a second crop, and till this under the same way. This will kill off most of the weeds in the area and add organic material to your new strawberry bed.

STRAWBERRY HARVEST

Date Set Out: _____

Variety, and Number of Each: _____

Where Obtained: _____

Details of Bed Preparation, Planting, Mulching: _____

_____

_____

Amounts Harvested

First Year	Second Year	Third Year
Variety Amount Date	Variety Amount Date	Variety Amount Date

Results
Which Varieties Are Best?

First Year: _____

Second Year: _____

Third Year: _____

In space below, sketch layout of plants, by variety, in your garden.

HERB HARVEST

(Under each variety, write down amount grown, whether enough or too much, how used, and whether it should be raised the following year. List all experiments with herbs.)

Variety: _____

_____

_____

Variety: _____

_____

_____

Variety: _____

_____

_____

Variety: _____

_____

_____

Variety: _____

_____

_____

Variety: _____

_____

_____

Variety: _____

_____

_____

Variety: _____

_____

_____

Variety: _____

_____

_____

Variety: _____

_____

_____

Herbs

There are hundreds of herbs to experiment with. First, you might like to try some of these. They are all easy to grow and a delight in the kitchen. They require little space and do well in so-so soil.

Basil: Sow directly in garden or start indoors. Basil has a spicy odor and taste that is fine with all vegetables, and especially salads with tomatoes. Also used in egg dishes and herb vinegars.

Borage: This annual grows up to three feet tall, so thin plants to a foot apart, after planting early in spring. Add young leaves to salad for a cucumber taste. Star-shaped flowers can be candied. Bees love to visit borage.

Chives: Plants of this perennial are easily started from seeds or by division of clumps of bulbs. Keep dividing them to keep the chives healthy. Can be started indoors, and can be potted for winter growing indoors. They're up early and ready to harvest early in the spring. When cutting them, cut to the base. And cut frequently, even if you must throw away some, to keep a supply of fresh, new leaves.

Dill: Raise this annual for dill pickles, or with broiled meats, fish sauces, and vegetables. Sow in early spring, and thin plants to four inches apart.

Parsley: A must for the kitchen. Can be started indoors or sown in the garden early in the spring. Rich in vitamins A and C, this biennial herb's green leaves and stems decorate as well as flavor potato dishes, sauces, and soups. Plant it as close to the kitchen as possible, so it will be available for nearly every meal. Easy to grow in pots on a windowsill.

Parsley

Chives

Basil

Borage

Dill

Other Garden Way Books

Garden Way's Joy of Gardening
by Dick Raymond

This is a how-to book, based on the popular television series, that's full of the same wealth of information, methods, tips, and tricks that Dick demonstrates on the show. With more than 600 color photos and illustrations. Trade paperback, $17.95. Hard cover, $25.

Garden Way's Joy of Gardening Cookbook
by Janet Ballantyne

A complete vegetable cookbook with more than 300 recipes (appetizers to main dishes and more) lavishly illustrated in 375 full-color photographs. Great harvesting hints, step-by-step, close-up photos of time- and flavor-saving techniques, tasty, unusual vegetable combinations, enticing finishing touches. Trade paperback, $17.95. Hard cover, $25.

These Garden Way Books are available wherever good books are sold, or may be ordered directly from Garden Way Publishing, Storey Communications, Inc., Dept 4121, Schoolhouse Road, Pownal, VT 05261. Please add $1.75 postage and handling if ordering one or both books.